RMA

Working with the Trauma of Rape and Sexual Violence

of related interest

Intimate Partner Sexual Violence
A Multidisciplinary Guide to Improving Services and
Support for Survivors of Rape and Abuse
Edited by Louise McOrmond-Plummer, Patricia
Easteal AM and Jennifer Y. Levy-Peck
Foreword by Raquel Kennedy Bergen
ISBN 978 1 84905 912 1
eISBN 978 0 85700 655 4

Counselling Adult Survivors of Child Sexual Abuse
Third Edition
Christiane Sanderson
ISBN 978 1 84310 335 6
eISBN 978 1 84642 532 5
ISBN 978 1 84985 014 8 [large print]

Violence Against Women
Current Theory and Practice in Domestic Abuse,
Sexual Violence and Exploitation
Edited by Nancy Lombard and Lesley McMillan
ISBN 978 1 84905 132 3
eISBN 978 0 85700 330 0

It's someone taking a part of you
A study of young women and sexual exploitation
Jenny J. Pearce with Mary Williams and Cristina Galvin
ISBN 978 1 90099 083 7
eISBN 978 1 90796 939 3

Narrative Therapy for Women Experiencing Domestic Violence
Supporting Women's Transitions from Abuse to Safety
Mary Allen
Foreword by Ravi K. Thiara
ISBN 978 1 84905 190 3
eISBN 978 0 85700 420 8

Take It as a Compliment
Maria Stoian
ISBN 978 1 84905 697 7
eISBN 978 0 85701 242 5

Working with the Trauma of Rape and Sexual Violence

A Guide for Professionals

Sue J. Daniels

Foreword by Ivan Tyrrell

Jessica Kingsley *Publishers*
London and Philadelphia

every effort has been made to trace copyright holders and to obtain their permission for the use of copyright material. The author and the publisher apologize for any omissions and would be grateful if notified of any acknowledgements that should be incorporated in future reprints or editions of this book.

Text on pages 209–10 is reproduced from Griffin and Tyrrell 2001 with kind permission from Human Givens Publishing.

Text on pages 40–2 is reproduced from Harry 1992 with kind permission from Sage College.

Text on pages 40–1 is reproduced from Donaldson 1990 with kind permission from The Brooke Russell Astor Reading Room.

Text on page 41 is reproduced from Porter 1986 with kind permission from Safer Society Press.

First published in 2017
by Jessica Kingsley Publishers
73 Collier Street
London N1 9BE, UK
and
400 Market Street, Suite 400
Philadelphia, PA 19106, USA
www.jkp.com

Library of Congress Cataloging in Publication Data
Names: Daniels, Sue J., author.
Title: Working with the trauma of rape and sexual violence : a guide for professionals / Sue J. Daniels.
Description: London ; Philadelphia : Jessica Kingsley Publishers, 2017. | Includes index.
Identifiers: LCCN 2016020554 | ISBN 9781785921117 (alk. paper)
Subjects: LCSH: Sexual abuse victims--Rehabilitation. | Sexual abuse victims--Services for. | Psychic trauma--Treatment.
Classification: LCC RC560.S44 D36 2017 | DDC 616.85/8369--dc23 LC record available at https://lccn.loc.gov/2016020554

British Library Cataloguing in Publication Data
A CIP catalogue record for this book is available from the British Library

ISBN 978 1 78592 111 7
eISBN 978 1 78450 375 8

Printed and bound in Great Britain

MIX
Paper from
responsible sources
FSC® C013056

Our prime purpose in this life is to help others and if you can't help them, at least don't hurt them.

Dalai Lama

I would like to dedicate this book to the courage, commitment and unique recovery of all clients past, present and future, from not only our service, but also from all other services available worldwide who are committed to working with victims of sexual violation.

What an honour it has been, to have been in a position to work with, learn from and to know each and every individual along their journey to post-trauma growth and recovery.

Contents

Foreword

An attractive and vivacious young woman came to see me because she was having panic attacks, flashbacks, and intrusive thoughts and exhibiting many other distressing symptoms of PTSD and living in a state of high anxiety and hypervigilance, particularly when in the presence of men who were attracted to her and despite the fact that she hoped for a normal, intimate and loving heterosexual relationship. This behaviour started after she was attacked and raped twice, a month apart, by two different strangers. Both men were caught and convicted.

Since the rapes and subsequent court cases she told me she had changed jobs several times because of her hysterical distress in the presence of men at work. Her psychological state led her to seek help from a clinical psychologist and a counsellor – encounters she had found disturbing, painful and useless. She hated talking about exactly what had happened. (Long-term talking therapy tends to reinforce trauma symptoms and embed them more deeply.)

Without knowing any more detail about the rapes than you have just read I detraumatised her in one session by using the rewind technique we at Human Givens College have refined and taught to thousands of people in the UK and abroad. (There are other techniques used for detraumatising people but our research found this the most reliable and safe way to do it.) When she returned a week later she confirmed that the anxiety had gone. She reported that after the session she had gone straight home, emptied her filing cabinet of all the papers relating to the two court cases, and thrown them in the dustbin, 'with no emotion at all'. She told me that prior to me seeing her, just opening the door of the room where the cabinet was situated made her burst into tears.

Having the ability to detraumatise people suffering from extreme anxiety symptoms is one of the most important skills any psychotherapist or counsellor possesses. This is because post traumatic stress disorder (PTSD) is often at the root of so many conditions that therapists are called upon to treat: including alcohol and drug addiction and other addictive behaviour, chronic depression, anger disorder, sexual and relationship problems and many other expressions of anxiety. Consequently I was pleased to see that, in Sue Daniels book, *Working with the Trauma of Rape and Sexual Violence*, she hasn't shied away from explaining how this dreadful cause of so much emotional pain – sexual violence – can be treated quickly in most cases.

It is impossible for a traumatised person to get their innate emotional needs met in a balanced way. For example, we all have an innate need for intimacy, but anyone who has been traumatised by violent rape will, at a fundamental level, find it hard to relax and enjoy intimacy with their loving partner because their alarm system is put on high alert when intimacy becomes sexual, however much they wish it were otherwise. The alarm cannot be turned off by an effort of will.

People become traumatised when they 'freeze' in the REM state during an event that their limbic system perceives as life-threatening. Because the REM state is also the programming state of the brain, whilst in that 'freeze state they are being programmed with the mass of information about what's happening as it's taken in through their senses. Traumatic symptoms occur later whenever the brain pattern-matches to any aspect of that stored information and it then fires off the fight-or-flight response. For example, a young woman I detraumatised had severe panic attacks whenever she saw a rubbish bin even though, intellectually, she knew bins are harmless. But she had had an experience where a particular rubbish bin was not harmless. Her leg had been blown off by a terrorist bomb that had been placed in a rubbish bin. Her limbic system couldn't take a chance that any rubbish bin she saw would not kill her and so pumped her system with adrenalin every time she saw a bin thereafter – until, that is, she was detraumatised, which only took a single session of therapy.

Psychological repair work over and above the rewind is often needed with people who have suffered sexual violence and abuse, particularly if it was sustained over a period of time and not just a single incident, but that should not begin until after they have been detraumatised. Sometimes, if they were in a good mental and emotional state before the violence occurred, they may only need to be detraumatised to pick up the pieces of their life again.

When properly applied, the rewind technique will almost always dissolve phobias, even serious ones, in one session. Likewise it will detraumatise disturbing flashbacks and cure the most severe post traumatic stress disorder (PTSD) caused by a single event, whatever the cause. With people who have a history of abuse, however, many sessions may be needed to deal separately with all the major incidents that traumatised them. Recent experience by experienced practitioners, however, has shown that it is sometimes possible to detraumatise many years of abuse and violent events in a single session. However, someone with such a history would generally still need to be seen a number of times, especially if the abuse had interfered with their normal psychological development.

The three advantages of this therapy

- It is *safe* (unlike critical incident debriefing).
- The rewind technique is *fast*.
- The rewind technique is *non-voyeuristic*. (The patient does not have to describe the event/events to you, a great advantage with traumatised victims of rape or sexual abuse.)

Whatever method used there are three elements to successful trauma treatment.

- The trauma template must be activated in the traumatised patient first – a degree of emotion about the abuse must be present.

- The person is then deeply relaxed using guided imagery.

- They are then dissociated from the memories of the abuse. The limbic system recodes the memory as non-threatening because the person is physiologically so deeply relaxed, it says to itself, as it were, "I'm so relaxed when reviewing these memories that there can be no danger here."

I think Sue has done a great service producing this well-researched book on such a grim subject. She describes the many forms of abusive behaviour and the symptoms they produce with great clarity and compassion. It will help many who struggle to heal the tortured souls of victims.

Ivan Tyrrell
Director of Human Givens College and co-author of
Human Givens: The new approach to emotional health and clear thinking

Acknowledgements

This publication has been the result of many years of continuous work with individuals who have been profoundly affected physically and psychologically by rape and sexual violence.

In the gradual transition from trauma therapist to author I have received much encouragement and support from a number of individuals, all of whom I am extremely grateful to for their time and inspiration. I would like to thank the following:

The current Jigsaw Post Trauma & Counselling Services Team, for giving me endless back up in so many ways during the setting up of the writing provision arm of Jigsaw.

Paul Fowler and Jay Mumby who have spent many hours of their time with me, both in person and on the telephone, going over the same things again and again. Jacqueline Martin for her friendship, understanding, essential input and for making me press the send button.

To all the team at Jessica Kingsley Publishers for believing in me, in this book and in its potential message to the hundreds of thousands of professionals who work with survivors.

And last, but never ever least, Mike, my wonderful husband, for always being there, quietly, patiently, waiting in the wings.

Author Note

The author does not accept responsibility for any of the materials, information and/or fictional case histories that some individuals may find distressing in this publication. Therefore the author disclaims and accepts no responsibility for any harm, injuries or unforeseen outcome as a result of any information contained within it. This book represents the true nature of rape and sexual violence and persons wishing to obtain an understanding of this sensitive issue may see and hear much worse than is featured within these pages.

Jigsaw Post Trauma & Counselling Services holds a current Crown Copyright Registration Licence of the Public Sector Information (PSI). (Licence number: C2008001507)

Much of the court procedure and legal information featured in this book is taken from websites containing Acts of English Law as and when they are provided, all of which is readily available to the general public, for example Sex Offences Acts and Home Office information.

Because of the accurate wording of these documents, it is impossible to write or impart this knowledge in any other way than to produce it in its entirety.

The author makes no representation, express or implied, with regard to the accuracy of the information contained in this publication and cannot accept any legal responsibility for any errors or omissions that may take place.

All government acts that have been cited or referred to are liable to change. The information contained within this publication is correct at the time of writing.

The reflective case histories featured in this publication are typical of many of the experiences of those who have been affected by sexual violation, encountered over the last two decades.

Introduction

From the sunshine of beautiful parks and sandy beaches to the darkened corners of children's bedrooms in the midnight hours, child abusers, sexual predators, rapists and violent sex offenders have permeated society leaving innocent victims psychologically and physically traumatised.

The effects of being raped and/or sexually violated can go right to the very core of a person's existence, likened to a metaphorical barbed splinter, and the more that person tries to ignore it, the sharper the barbs become and the deeper the splinter goes, taking with it a myriad of emotions and psychological pain.

I have worked with hundreds of clients who have not only been the victim of a sexual violation but then disbelieved, dismissed, judged or blamed by someone they later confided in. This might have been a friend, family member, or worse still, a professional, such as a counsellor, teacher, doctor, police officer, hospital employee, barrister, solicitor, medical examiner and/or any others involved with a survivor. This has the power of actually making the person feel worse about themselves and about the incident.

In writing this book I hope at the very least to raise awareness of the difficulties that such negative responses can cause for an individual who has found themselves a target of sexual violation of any kind.

I have also met some of the most non-judgemental and empathic professionals along the way including high court judges, police officers at every rank, military personnel, solicitors, rape crisis centre workers, doctors, independent sexual violence advisors (ISVAs), counsellors and many others, who have excelled in the aftercare of both male and female victims of sexual violence in terms of their physical, psychological and practical post trauma care.

If your work puts you in touch with those who have experienced rape and/or sexual violation of any kind, this book may help you to understand the psychological and physical manifestations that victims are often left to live with.

I can only write what I hear and encounter on a regular basis and from the experiences that have been shared with me over the years. To have been able to write this book freely and honestly about how I perceive the way survivors of sexual violation should be treated has been very special indeed.

It is my ultimate hope that this publication may convey perhaps a new understanding, opening up new possibilities of working with those who have had to endure the aftermath of vile and twisted behaviours perpetrated upon them, very often by the people who were supposed to love and protect them.

Prologue

Imagine for a moment that you are female, 29 years old, happy go lucky and just love to live life to the full. You work hard at your job, and it's five o'clock on a Friday. You've just finished a gruelling 40-hour week, and you're planning on a night out with some old friends who you've not seen for a while. You get to the car park, dump your work bag in the boot along with your work jacket, get in your car and off you go home, the same routine as every other normal Friday evening.

Once you are at home you open your door, pick up the mail, check the answer machine and, as you lock your door, you feed the cat, put the kettle on and sit down to read your mail. You have received mostly bills, which you put to one side, but by now the cat is meowing at the door to go out, and you notice she must have cut herself because of the blood spots on the white kitchen floor tiles. Thinking no more you check the cat's paws, let her outside and wipe up the blood. Coffee digested you decide to have a long hot bath and pamper yourself before getting ready for the evening out. You are excited to be seeing your old friends and have lots to catch up on.

You decide that the new black jeans should be okay with a cream ruffle blouse, and so you lay them out on the bed and start to run your bath. The scent of a coconut bath bomb fills the air, and you gently sing along to yourself gathering your underwear from the radiator, left there to dry earlier. After having washed your hair you put it up in a towel and get undressed to ease yourself into the luscious bath, just as you've done many times before.

Laying back in the bath you close your eyes, starting to relax into a beautiful daydream state, when all of a sudden you are brought back to earth by the sound of a gentle click from the back bedroom.

Eyes wide open now you quickly sit up and turn around to see if you can see around the door; you wait a while and for some unknown ridiculous reason you call out to see if anyone answers. No answer, so you think about continuing to relax but you are now too unsettled so decide to get washed and get out of the bath.

Dried now, in your bathrobe, you go to check the back bedroom, and as you do so, suddenly a hand grabs your wrist and spins you around ramming you up against the wall. It's your sister's husband; he's drunk and angry and he tells you he is going to get what he wants whether you like it or not. He tells you that you are no better than him and looking down your nose at him ends now. You have been terrified of this violent aggressive man since you were six years old, and right now you are absolutely petrified. It feels like all of this is happening in slow motion; he has already split your lip, and you can taste the blood as well as the smell of his rancid body odour, thick with smoke and beer.

He grabs your hair and throws you onto the bed raping you violently, slapping, punching and biting at your skin intermittently.

Right now adrenaline has been released from your adrenal glands (situated above your kidneys).

Red blood cells flood to carry oxygen – blood is diverted to wherever it is needed. Your breathing has become rapid to provide you with more energy. Your lungs have dilated to give you more oxygen.

Your sweating has increased, and you want to vomit, but you can't. You need the toilet badly, which is your body's way of making your body lighter for purposes of flight. Your muscles have tightened and you are like a coiled spring. Your blood pressure is up, and apart from the blood seeping from the split in your lip your mouth is very dry.

All of this is happening to you in a split second, even though it feels and seems much longer. The silence in your head is deafening as you endure this torture by a man who has known you since you had your first bicycle. By now you are in so much pain. Your eyes feel like they are bleeding. You are dizzy where he's punched you in your head.

You play dead now, because from some primal instinctive response, you know that this is your only real defence, and as your lifeless body drops to the floor from the bed he has thrown you onto, you can hear him shouting at you to wake up, your face taking the pain as he continues slapping you across the face again and again.

You are now on the ceiling looking down, watching him revile you in many ways, but you can also hear voices outside calling your name fading in and out, through the letterbox maybe, or up to the window. You are still playing dead, but panic sets in again, allowing all the changes that are already occurring within your body to start to increase all over again as you think he is surely going to kill you.

Then, still too terrified to open your eyes, you hear footsteps running down the stairs, the back door slamming shut, voices shouting echo throughout your house from outside and again you just want to go to sleep.

'It's okay. It's only me, Sheila from next door but one, lovey. Keep your eyes open, lovey. Ambulance is on its way.' You talk, but you don't know what you are saying. It's as if someone else is speaking for you.

Two paramedics rush into the room and call you by your name…

1

The Traumatic Effects of Rape and Sexual Violence

Rape and sexual assault are not about sex or a sexual relationship. They are serious crimes about power, control, humiliation and domination.

The word rape originates from the Latin verb *rapere*: to seize or to take by force. The Latin term for the act of rape itself is *raptus*. Originally it had no sexual connotation, and is still used generically in English.

The history of rape and the revisions of its meaning are multifaceted to say the least. The trauma of a rape or other sexual attack can set off a sequence of survival skills which are crucial and necessary at the time of attack, but which usually become less crucial or effective with time. Sometimes targets of rape become stuck in distorted, unfamiliar behaviours when their pain is not acknowledged, heard, respected or understood.

Self-blame can be further embedded by the persons' story being put down or dismissed, or worse still, their actions, choice of clothing, lifestyle and social status judged by others. These are just some of the forms of secondary wounding which keep the target trapped within their own private nightmare, experiencing symptoms such as flashbacks and/or panic attacks, which may come on soon after the sexual violation or years later.

Rape is a physical, sexual assault involving non-consensual use of the sexual organs of another person's body. The perpetrator can be of either gender as can their target. In general, rape is considered as one of the most serious sex crimes and can be difficult to prosecute, hence the need and importance of so many SARCs (Sexual Assault Referral Centres) and excellent Rape Crisis organisations available in many countries.

The purpose of a well-managed SARC is to give victims an opportunity to have forensic testing carried out in a safe and hermetically sealed environment and for the police to obtain as much 'pure' evidence as possible in order to prosecute the sexual offender. To retain evidence is not always the first thought on a person's mind when they have just been sexually violated by one or a number of perpetrators. Generally their first thought is to scrub themselves clean, innocently washing away any crucial evidence.

For those of us who are likely to come into contact with someone who has been subjected to rape and/or sexual violence, it may help to understand how others have reacted in similar circumstances, and how you can work with a person to assist normal healing and recovery.

Post-traumatic stress disorder (PTSD) is an automatic response to being exposed to a traumatic experience which is considered to be life threatening. In cases of rape and sexual violence it is referred to as post-traumatic rape syndrome. It is a normal human emotional reaction to an abnormal situation.

Everyone reacts differently to different situations and it doesn't have to be a life-threatening experience for someone to respond in this way. It just has to be perceived by the person affected as a traumatic event. It is a terrifying experience, but with the correct attention, it is possible to make a full and complete recovery.

PTSD affects millions of people, and many attempt to mask it in different ways, using a variety of supports such as alcohol, drugs, over-working and in endless other ways. It is only when asking for help that the condition may be recognised and treated.

It is not rare, unusual or weak to have PTSD. It is not about what is wrong with a person; it is about what happened to them.

The aftermath of the crime of rape has the power to leave a person in a state of imbalance and emotional turmoil. Physical sensations vary from person to person. Some people respond immediately and some bury the incident/s deep down for many years. Moods can change, and the person may find it difficult to talk about or explain. Day-to-day functioning can become almost impossible and people find that they compensate in other ways.

Victims of rape are more often severely traumatised by the assault, and may have difficulty functioning at their 'normal' day-to-day level prior to the assault, with disruption of concentration, sleeping patterns and eating habits as just a few examples. Response may play out in varying ways, either expressively or in a controlled way, which occurs when the victim appears to be quite calm and rational about the situation, even if facing severe internal turmoil.

There is no single response to rape; every individual deals with their emotions differently.

Potential feelings and emotional responses experienced by a target of rape and/or sexual violence are shown in in Table 1.1.

Table 1.1 Emotional responses to rape and/or sexual violence

Triggered fear	Reliving and feeling the assault in the body in the sleeping and waking state (abreaction)
	Avoidance of any thoughts, feelings or places that remind the victim of the assault
	A vast need to forget what happened and move on with life. Anxiety about things that weren't previously there or apparent. Difficulty sleeping and staying asleep or focussing and concentrating on one thing
	Fear of damage to self or loved ones
	Not being believed – made to look like a liar or attention seeker
	Repeat attacks – hypervigilance
	Of breaking down or losing control in front of others
	Of losing control in front of others
Sadness	For injury and loss of every kind
	Why me?
	For the perpetrator (familial) in some cases
	Self-blaming – often leading to depression and anxiety
	For putting family and friends through vicarious trauma at having to listen to the details. Memories of the incident may be shady or seem unreal

Shame	Feeling as if thoughts are not owned, as if brain has been taken over and thinking time interrupted
	Dissociation and detachment
	If the survivor was drugged, the attack may have been filmed – constant imaginings of the implications of this
	For being exposed as needing help
	For not being able to defend one's self
	The location of the physical injuries, anal, vaginal or both
	Having to endure the indignation of a forensic medical examination (often with a male practitioner)
Helplessness	Feeling in a daze or detached – like being in a dream or feeling of complete disorientation
	Going into trance-like states – statue like
	Not understanding
	Confusion
	How did it happen?
	Out of control
	Having no say in what was happening
	Not being able to defend oneself
Anger	At the perpetrator and his/her vileness
	At not being strong enough to overcome the perpetrator
	The injustice and audacity of the attack
	How men and women are so unequal when it comes to being sexually overpowered
	At the lack of proper understanding of the profundity of such an attack

Trauma response

Trauma response is what happens when a part of the brain reacts to a life-threatening or life-endangering event. It is the body's primitive reaction, which sets off the flight, fight or freeze reaction. It is a normal response to danger, and its main function is to keep us alive.

The fight, flight or freeze response prepares us to act in many situations and in the case of a sexual attack it gets us ready to either fight the sexual predator or to escape if that's a possibility. The freeze response is when we can neither escape nor fight, and in order to survive, the part of the brain called the amygdala holds on to every detail of the attack.

Acting like a constant bodyguard, it keeps the person on high alert in case of further attack. This high alert mechanism is the main element that triggers panic attacks and flashbacks – reminding the person affected every time he/she recognises a signal that replicates the attack or environmental reminders at the time of the attack. A basic understanding of the fight, flight or freeze response is crucial to understanding the trauma response and the unprocessed information that many of those affected by rape and/or sexual violence are forced to live with.

As illustrated briefly in the prologue, the human body, when faced with a life-threatening situation, will respond in some or all of the following ways:

- Adrenaline is released from the adrenal glands (situated above the kidneys).

- Red blood cells flood to carry oxygen. Blood is diverted to wherever it is needed.

- The brain feels fogged – unable to focus on anything but fighting or fleeing.

- Breathing becomes faster to provide more energy, and we are able to take in more oxygen which is then transferred into the blood stream.

- Lungs dilate to get more oxygen.

- Sweating allows the body to cool down after being heated up so suddenly.

- Vomiting may occur in readiness to make us lighter.

- Bowels become loose in readiness to make us lighter.

- Excessive urination may occur in readiness to make us lighter.

- Muscles tighten, which can be painful, in readiness to escape or fight.

- The heart beat speeds up – our blood pressure goes up giving more blood to the muscles in readiness to run or defend ourselves.

- The mouth dries up, because we don't need the saliva.

All of the above occur in a split second, and it is only after the incident when the body calms down that the unprocessed information can begin to be worked with, if the person seeks assistance.

This famous flight or fight response system is known by many people in many walks of life. However, the freeze response is not so well known, nor is the fact that it is the most dangerous of the responses. This is because it obstructs any reaction, leaving the victim motionless and unable to respond at all. Worse than this, the freeze response can lead directly to post-traumatic stress disorder and related symptoms.

Post-traumatic stress disorder

Working with clients who have been subjected to rape and sexual violence can be extremely difficult. It is a fragile process that differs from person to person. The physical wounds can be healed, however, the inner pain, the psychological agony that people can't see, often takes the longest to work through. But it can be done and millions of those affected live normal lives because of the excellent psychological processing interventions, available across the globe.

There are a number of conditions that are considered crucial in establishing whether or not a person is suffering from post-traumatic stress disorder (PTSD). This condition is determined by factors such as exposure to the event/s, response, and consequences for the individual affected. These can present as minimal, such as temporary sleep disturbance, or they can be further reaching, influencing thoughts, feelings and behaviours.

Symptoms of this may present as continually ruminating over the event so that it takes up valuable thinking time; individuals may experience a sense of overwhelming fear, intrusive images, thoughts, colours, smells and memories connected with the incident.

Avoidance plays a part with some people, carefully avoiding talking, thinking or allowing triggers into their life that remind them of the assault.

After being attacked and invaded internally, in terms of rape or sexual violation, the body as well as the brain remembers every second of the assault, hardwired to react to external and/or internal reminders. If a person has been exposed to an incident in which their life was threatened, their brain and body then works instinctively to keep them safe by reminding them of the dangers faced on that day, whether that was being involved or as a witness. It is a perfectly normal response and is in fact, the body keeping itself safe from further harm.

Example

Some years ago I worked with a client who had been sexually violated by a male masseur, during a massage treatment whilst on holiday in Greece. This had happened to her approximately three years previously and the client stated that although she had thought she had been able to move on from it, she presented with having intermittent 'funny turns', as she called them.

We worked with the Three Point Turnaround System© (Appendix 10) taking a timeline of the assault. The client stated that at certain times during her present, normal day to day functioning, she would feel panicky and struggled to catch her breath.

After much further exploration, it emerged that the mustard yellow colour of a certain metal road sign which was affixed on the route that the client took twice each day for her daughter's school run, was the exact same shade as the colour of the masseur's t-shirt, the one who had sexually violated her. This was her body and brain reminding her of a threat to her life; however subtle, it served only to protect her. Although it did not feel like it for the client, this was a perfectly normal response, reminding her and keeping her safe.

Using eye movement desensitising reprocessing (EMDR) combined with The Rewind Technique (Appendix 9) over a six week period, the client was able to process all of the details as we worked extensively and specifically with her cognitive, kinaesthetic, visual, olfactory and gustatory senses. In brief, the client completed her therapy sessions stating that she no longer experienced the 'funny turns' that had previously affected her day to day routines.

Post-traumatic stress disorder is a term that was more commonly associated with the military, its historic term being 'shell shock'. Sadly the condition was not fully understood and often to the detriment of those suffering from it, were labelled as absconders, cowards, having lack of moral fibre (LMF), stress and burn out.

The truth is that those suffering from the post trauma (after wound) of rape and/or sexual violence are actually living in their own private hell, in their unique and all-encompassing prison. The condition called rape-related post-traumatic stress disorder (RR-PTSD) is a reaction to being exposed to sexual violation of any kind, whether as an adult or as a child. RR-PTSD is not rare. It is not unusual, nor is it is weak to experience the condition.

Amygdala: the brain alarm system to ensure survival

After a rape or sexual violation occurs, the emotional reaction can remain encoded in the amygdala, where it stays like a template, a reminder if needed in a similar situation.

It is a perfectly normal response, keeping us safe from similar danger. With the many reprocessing interventions available, it is possible to 'override' this process allowing the traumatic information to be processed in the waking state safely and effectively.

Defining rape

Rape is the invasion of the most private and sacred part of a person's being: an invasion like a sharply embedded barbed, deeply embedded splinter. Afterwards, the more a victim is 'forced' to heal within a time limit, the sharper the barbs become as the already screaming splinter deepens day by day.

There are many definitions of rape; however, the people most qualified to create this definition are victims themselves. All names in the following definitions have been changed to protect the identity of those affected.

Victim 1: Niamh

It was the end of my life as I knew it and the start of a nightmare that I felt I may never wake up from. The rapist walks free, and me, well, I have to live every day with the memory of what he did to me.

Judgements, questions, non-believers and being injured over and over again by people's inability to understand the depth of this horror. Not enough evidence they said – my mental health and the cost to the NHS since, isn't that evidence enough?

Victim 2: Julia

For me, the simplest way to define rape would be to describe it as a vicious assault on every sense, leaving deep, vivid scarring to both mind and body.

The SIGHT of the attacker, a face that will be forever imprinted on my mind. The SOUND of my own voice, pleading for it to stop, begging to be left alive.

The TASTE and SMELL of the attacker, which clings for days, even weeks. No matter how many times I scrub myself to try and make it go away.

The FEEL of my own body being used, abused, damaged and violated in the most painful and degrading way.

Victim 3: Anna

Rape scars you for life, but on the inside, where no one can see, you are left like a broken jigsaw, trying to make sense of the pieces that you are left with. To somehow put them back together in an order that feels okay to bear and to live with. Rape leaves a victim forever vulnerable like an open sore that won't heal.

Victim 4: Jonty

A most harrowing experience or degradation resulting in overwhelming isolation and inability to live normally ever again. Unable to speak to people in case they know or judge me as a victim. Fear that the gang may seek me out and find me – terror in every part of my body, always in all ways.

Victim 5: Victoria

Loss of life as I knew it, loss of friends, family and everyone I held dear but mostly loss of my once-clear brain function.

Victim 6: Colin

The single most degrading and sick act imaginable, forever leaving its imprint on the victim.

Secondary injury/wounding

This can occur in many ways in the aftermath of the trauma of rape, for example:

- a rape victim who visits a practitioner and is asked to be honest with him/herself and to admit what he/she had done to attract his/her attacker

- not being believed by the person the victim has confided in

- on first contact with an untrained police officer, being told that it happened so long ago, why would you want to rake it all up now?

- a court case not being heard or not enough evidence, listed as a 'no crime' without explanation

- a perpetrator not being charged and set free (striking fear into the victim of retribution or repeat attack)

- being arrested for perverting the course of justice if no evidence is found by police, the case being 'no crimed' and giving the message to victim that it did not really happen

- being told that as there were no witnesses there could be no case to answer.

Rape can have serious consequences affecting an individual for the rest of their life, if their physiological unprocessed traumatic response is not addressed adequately, carefully and effectively. The most extreme cases may end in suicide. Genuine people affected by rape are not attention seekers. They are living in constant turmoil, needing psychological assistance to work through a traumatic incident. They are not mad; they are responding 'normally' to a completely abnormal and often harrowing event in their life.

Generic counselling and talking therapy may help in a supportive role, but in reality, this type of assistance can actually further embed the already debilitating effects. If professionals can gain even some basic knowledge about how traumatic incident effects the human brain, the level of support without further damage instantly increases greatly. This allows the individual to process the incident safely for their recovery.

Victims of rape, whether male or female, usually manifest some elements of rape-related post-traumatic stress disorder (RR-PTSD), a form of PTSD. Apart from a small number of therapists and professionals specialising in sexual assault cases, few professionals are familiar with the symptoms and treatment of RR-PTSD. To work without the competency to do so can further harm those who may have come to you for assistance.

Rape-related post-traumatic stress disorder

There are many symptoms stated within the diagnostic criteria for post-traumatic stress disorder; however, those that primarily stand out for victims of rape are:

- random intrusive thoughts, images and feelings about the attack, causing the victim to re-experience what happened

- isolation, not wanting to socialise or talk to anyone about the attack

- normalising or avoiding the most traumatic elements of the attack

- change of personality, irritability, misdirected anger and bouts of rage.

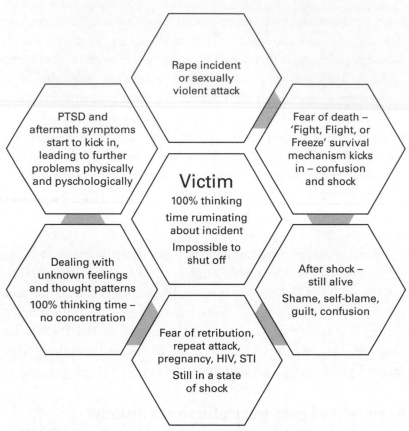

Figure 1.1 Stranger, gang or singular rape: incident cycle of consequence

In addition to the cycle of consequence shown in Figure 1.1 some of the further issues to deal with if the rape incident is reported to the police are shown in Figure 1.2.

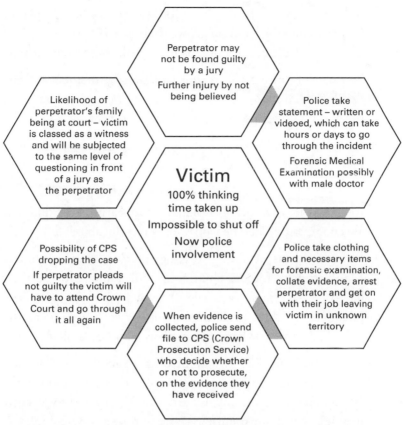

Figure 1.2 Stranger, gang or singular rape: incident cycle of consequence if reported to the police

Satanic and ritual abuse

Of all the cases we work with as professionals, some of the hardest histories to understand are from clients who have suffered satanic or ritual abuse from childhood. The atrocities that they have suffered, often from their own parents and relations, can sometimes seem unreal and difficult to hear.

Satanic ritual abuse, also known as SRA, includes the following types of abuse:

- Conditioning the child into believing that he/she is a child of the devil. This can stay with a person for life.

- Rejection by a belief in God – conditioning blame. Conditioning the child to believe they are to blame as they are ultimately bad and deserving of any and all abuse against them.

- Normalising incest and sexual violation by members of the family. Conditioning of the child leads to their acceptance of the abuse, and they grow up unaware of this being wrong.

- Emotional conditioning and abuse. For example, the child may be given toys at Christmas and birthdays only to have them immediately taken away.

- Keeping the child socially isolated, by appearing to be different at school, so that he/she won't tell about the abuse.

- Physical abuse, beating, cutting and/or drawing blood. Bloodletting – forcing children to kill animals to use their blood – sacrificing animals. Keeping the child/children prisoner/s in their own home – isolating. Speaking to the child in a particular language, such as Latin or similar.

- Performing cult-like rituals involving blood smearing and rape of children, with the perpetrator often dressed in various frightening costumes. Children are terrified into silence, unable to think for themselves and almost always completely unable to make decisions in later life.

- There are cases where children have been born specifically to be abused in this way.

Here I include some true testimonies from clients who have given their written permission to allow publication (I have changed their names, gender and all identities to protect them further).

Olive

My Auntie said 'God will save you.' How shit is that? They make you naked in the church. They make you eat raw meat as a sacrifice and then they make you drink blood to reject the devil from you. I was terrified for all of my life, told I was a devil child and that to be so brutally abused in so many ways by so many men was the only way to force the devil out of me. I still think about the textures they put in my mouth, I cannot eat anything like it, even now.

I have always felt unclean, never known love nor do I want to, most of the time I just want to not live this horror of an existence. To not be frightened, I spend all of my days indoors with the lights on and the curtains closed. I bathe at least six times a day. I use bleach and all number of detergents to try and wash their vileness from me.

Slowly though, with help, going through the worst memories and being heard allowed me to put them to rest and I am beginning to breathe and my hope is that I can find my voice. I want to feel free enough to go outside, to feel the rain on my skin and the warmth of the sun on my head. That's all, that's all I want even for just one day.

Paul

My first memory is being led into a church. On reflection it was more like a sort of makeshift church in an old village hall. I can still smell the mustiness. In front of at least 30 others, two men dressed in robes undressed me, and I will never forget the pain as they violated my scrawny six-year-old body. They made me drink blood, which they told me was the blood of Christ and that this treatment of me was the only way to keep the devil out of me.

I ran away many times and was always brought home. It was my father who took me to this place, and each time the police or authorities brought me home, he beat me to within an inch of my life after they had gone.

He told me I wasn't worthy of attention and would lock me in my room for days on end without food. I had a dog's bowl of water. I had no toys or anything. My room was filthy. I remember there being two brick walls showing under the plaster, and old paper was hanging off the other walls. Sometimes he would come and get me to take me to the church place, and other times he would send men up to my room to abuse me. It was always in the name of God though, always.

Nigel

I was owned by my uncle. He had 'claimed' me apparently when I was just three years old. I think I was lucky, because I had a magical way of looking down on the abuse from above. The therapist calls it dissociation, but whatever it was, it helped me detach from the reality of what was happening.

My uncle was a teacher at our Sunday school choir. He would take me to their meetings after choir practice with three other boys. We were ritually subjected to sadistic assaults, physically, emotionally and sexually at every level of depravity that one human can bestow upon another. It was sick and twisted and we were all always terrified. Even now that the abusers are dead and buried, I can't be in the same location as where it happened, I'm far enough away geographically, but my mind is often back there and I still don't sleep properly.

I have been sectioned eleven times and you know what, until now, I've never felt believed or understood. My experience was never validated, just covered up with drugs or people telling me what was best for me. So, no different to the abusers really, just in a different form. Now I am on a road of recovery of sorts. I've been able to connect with that little boy who was abused and tell him just how much he really is worth.

I may never recover, but with help I am starting to look forward instead of back. I see the new fresh road ahead and not the filthy path behind. I am looking forward yes, to a future I didn't dare believe could be possible.

Sarah

Church, church, church, always the bloody church. My mother was obsessed with sending me there. She's dead now, and I will never know if she actually knew about what they did to me on a Sunday morning and on a Tuesday evening after school, in that fucking church.

I must have been seven years old when it first started. They would strip me naked, and the big priest would start by laying me out on a sort of table and raping me. There are no words to describe the pain of the rape let alone the shame and humiliation. When he'd finished, he would pass me round while the others watched. Sometimes they would make me do things to them and then after, they would beat me with a belt, for doing it, as if I'd had a choice! The worst thing I could have done was to not cry, because then they just carried on beating me till I did cry, but I had detached. I was numb to the pain, the humiliation, it really was as if I was watching from the side or up above. The whole thing was horrific and I am only glad that I have finally found some kind of way of working through what happened.

Any kind of sexual interaction with children, whether it is wrapped up in religion or as ritual, satanic cult or whatever the abusers or media choose to call it, is still child abuse, sadistic sexual assault and nothing more than an excuse for grown men and sometimes women to get their kicks from having sex with children.

In fact, it seems, the more power they are able to exert over innocent children and the more terror they can instil, the better they like it. The children on the other hand, have no choice, no say and no voice at all. The repercussions for those affected stay with them throughout their lives, triggered by almost anything in their day to day existence.

2

Male Rape, Sexual Assault and Violence

'Men cannot be raped.' This statement is completely untrue; men can be raped and are vulnerable in the same way as women, both physically and emotionally. Male rape and sexual assault is not a new issue; it is only that we as a society have become more aware of its occurrence, which in part is due to excellent online and telephone services such as ChildLine and the endless floodgates that have opened. This has resulted in the disclosure of many high profile sexual perpetrators who have abused male children in schools, colleges, children's homes, church organisations and so on.

Neither sexual desire nor sexual deprivation is the primary motivating force behind sexual assault. It is not about sexual gratification, but rather a sexual aggressor using somebody else as a means of expressing power and control. Much has been written about the psychological trauma associated with the rape of female targets; while less research has been conducted about male rape, case research suggests that males also commonly experience many of the reactions that females experience.

History

The rape of males was more widely documented in ancient times. Several of the legends in Greek mythology involved abductions and sexual assaults of males by other males or gods. The rape of a defeated male enemy was considered the special right of the victorious soldier in some societies and was a signal of the totality of the defeat. There was a widespread belief that a male who was sexually penetrated, even if it was by forced sexual assault, thus 'lost his manhood' and could no longer be a warrior or ruler. Gang rape of a male was considered an ultimate form of punishment and, as such, was known to the Romans as punishment for adultery and the Persians and Iranians as punishment for violation of the sanctity of the harem (Donaldson 1990).

Prison rape

Many people believe that the majority of male rape occurs in prison. However, there is research which shatters this myth. A study of incarcerated and non-incarcerated male rape victims in Tennessee concluded that the similarities between these two groups would suggest that the sexual assault of men may not be due to conditions unique to a prison and that all men are potential victims (Lipscomb 1992).

Boys and teenagers

Boys in their early and mid-teens are more likely to be victimised than older males (studies indicate a median victim age of 17). The form of assault usually involves penetration of the victim anally and/or orally, rather than stimulation of the victim's penis. Gang rape is more common in cases involving male victims than those involving female victims. Also, multiple sexual acts are more likely to be demanded, weapons are more likely to be displayed and used, and physical injury is more likely to occur, with the injuries that do occur being more serious than with injured female rape victims (Porter 1986).

Male rape as an act of anti-gay violence

Unfortunately, incidents of anti-gay violence also include forcible rape, either oral or anal. Attackers frequently use verbal harassment and name calling during such a sexual assault. Given the context of coercion, however, such technically homosexual acts seem to imply no homosexuality on the part of the offenders. The victim serves, both physically and symbolically, as a 'vehicle for the sexual status needs of the offenders in the course of recreational violence' (Harry 1992, p.115).

Physical and emotional responses of male sexual violation

These include the following:

- denial and/or guilt

- shame or humiliation

- fear and a feeling of loss of control

- loss of self-respect

- flashbacks to the attack

- anger and anxiety

- retaliation fantasies (sometimes shocking the victim with their graphic violence)

- nervous or compulsive behaviour

- depression and mood swings

- withdrawal from relationships

- changes in sexual activity.

Just as for females, targets of male rape are usually well advised to consult with a practitioner who is knowledgeable in the area of RR-PTSD and preferably a specialist in this area, rather than relying on general counselling or support services and resources.

Working with rape and sexual violence puts a person in touch with some of the most sickening acts one person can do to another. The effects that rape and/or sexual assault can have on a man are in many ways similar to those that affect a woman, and as we have previously mentioned, the response of society is markedly different. Men are seen as strong protectors, capable of defending themselves and those that they care about.

When male rape occurs, feelings of shame, guilt, bewilderment and disbelief often lead to a change in self-esteem. Frequently men may feel unable to express their anger and rage at what has happened to them and turn it in on themselves or others.

It is only by bringing these issues out into the open and encouraging male targets of rape to discuss them that we can hope to change society's attitudes so that male rape is seen as the same violent crime as female rape.

3

Drug Facilitated Sexual Assault (DFSA)

Drug facilitated sexual assault (DFSA) is a doubly cowardly act and happens when a perpetrator spikes or contaminates an intended target's drink with a drug that will cause them to become defenceless.

Because most DFSA drugs dissolve quickly and can be produced as colourless, odourless and tasteless, a person can ingest one unknowingly. The drugs are easily added to flavoured drinks without the person's knowledge. Within ten to twenty minutes that person can become ill, disorientated or very sleepy, unable to move and/or think clearly. They are rendered physically helpless, unable to refuse (or consent) to sexual intercourse. If the drink contains alcohol, then the effects of the drugs can be intensified. The devastating consequences can last anywhere from two to twenty-four hours, leaving an unsuspecting target incapable of remembering what has happened.

This kind of sexual predator uses drugs as a way to overpower their target of assault in order to sedate them, causing them to be incapacitated and unable to fight back, often compensating for their own sexual inadequacies. Unfortunately, these drugs are easily accessible. Some are legal for use for other purposes and are therefore readily available and inexpensive.

There are many different types of drugs used to assist a sexual assault which, as previously described, is any type of sexual activity that a person does not agree to, including inappropriate touching, vaginal/anal penetration, sexual intercourse, rape, and/or attempted rape.

The following will give you information about those drugs that are commonly used. Alcohol can be just as dangerous, for example slipping a small amount of vodka into a pint of lager or beer over a period of time can have a quite serious effect in terms of rendering the intended target incapacitated. In addition, with the trend in today's society for the excessive consumption of alcohol, it is important to remember that drinking alcohol to excess can also cause many of the same sedative effects of the drugs discussed in this chapter.

Rohypnol

Rohypnol (Flunitrazepam) is known to induce anterograde amnesia in the right dosage. Victims of sexual assault who have been given this drug are unable to remember certain events that they have experienced whilst under its influence. It is difficult to estimate how many Rohypnol-facilitated rapes have actually occurred, because more often than not, by the time forensic samples are collected the drug has left the body resulting in difficulty in obtaining evidence.

Urine samples need to be taken within 72 hours for a trace to be evident through sensitive analysis. Having said this, it is now possible to detect Rohypnol for up to one month by taking a hair sample.

Side effects and withdrawal symptoms of Rohypnol

Every medication contains chemicals that can cause side effects or adverse reactions. Some side effects are physical, such as nausea or blurred vision, while others can affect mood and emotions.

Rohypnol withdrawal symptoms may include abdominal pains, aching, agoraphobia, anxiety, blurred vision, body vibrations, changes in perception, diarrhoea, distended abdomen, feeling of unreality, flu-like symptoms, flatulence, food cravings, hair loss, heart palpitations, heavy limbs, increased allergies, increased sense of smell, insomnia, lethargy, loss of balance, metallic taste, muscle spasms, nightmares, panic attacks, paranoia, persistent and unpleasant memories, severe headaches, shaking, short-term memory loss, sore mouth and tongue, sound and light sensitivity, speech difficulties, sweating, suicidal thoughts, tinnitus, unusual sensitivity and fear.

Gamma Hydroxybutyrate

Gamma Hydroxybutyrate (GHB) (powder, tablet and liquid) is a drug that has been referred to in the media as a 'date rape drug', in much the same way as alcohol and Rohypnol, as it is colourless and odourless and has been described as 'very easy to add to drinks'.

GHB has been used in many cases of drug-related sexual assault, usually when the victim is vulnerable due to intoxication with a sedative, generally alcohol or more rarely cannabis, and as such is less likely to notice a strange taste to his or her drink.

Side effects and withdrawal symptoms of GHB

These include intoxication, difficulty concentrating, increased energy, happiness, talking and desire to socialise, feeling affectionate and playful, sensuality, enhanced sexual experience, muscle relaxation, loss of coordination due to loss of muscle tone, loss of gag reflex, nausea, vomiting, headaches, drowsiness, dizziness, amnesia, loss of muscle control, respiratory problems, loss of consciousness, being conscious but unable to move, sedation, desire to sleep, rambling, incoherent speech, slurred speech, giddiness, silliness, difficulty thinking, passing out and death – especially when combined with alcohol or other drugs – nausea (withdrawal), insomnia (withdrawal), anxiety, tremors (withdrawal) and sweating (withdrawal).

GHB's intoxicating effects begin ten to twenty minutes after the drug is taken. The effects typically last up to four hours, depending on the dosage.

Ketamine

Ketamine, also known as 'Special K', is sold in either powdered or liquid form. In powdered form, its appearance is similar to that of pharmaceutical grade cocaine. It can be injected or placed in beverages. It is also possible to smoke the drug in a joint or pipe, usually mixed with marijuana and tobacco. The smoke has a distinctive bitter taste, but the effects of the high hit much faster than when inhaled.

Oral use usually requires more material, but results in a longer trip. However, when administered orally, ketamine goes straight to the liver, where it is processed into nor ketamine. This creates a numbness and difficulty to walk, talk or move around. It takes only ten to fifteen seconds for the dose to take effect, which is why it is so dangerous when used to facilitate a sexual assault.

A main characteristic of ketamine is a stupor similar to extreme drunkenness. This is commonly known as 'being in the K-hole'. Side effects and withdrawal symptoms of ketamine include increased heart rate, slurred speech, feeling of paralysis, nausea, inability to move, hallucination, numbness, impaired attention, memory and learning ability, delirium, amnesia, impaired motor function, high blood pressure, depression and potentially fatal respiratory problems at higher doses.

An overdose of ketamine will knock a person out as if in an operating theatre. If repeatedly taken in large doses, ketamine can induce unconsciousness and failure of the cardiovascular system, leading to death. There have been a number of ketamine-related deaths.

Ketamine was classified as a Class C drug under the Drugs Act 2005, with the legislation taking effect from 1 January 2006. This has now been amended and came into force on 10 June 2014 under amendment order reference; Circular 008/2014: changes to The Misuse of Drugs Act 1971.

4

Childhood Sexual Abuse, Sibling Sexually Abusive Behaviours and Grooming and Conditioning Behaviours

A common trait of child sexual abusers has always been their access to children, authorised or otherwise. Sexual predators who prey on children almost always put themselves in positions of authority or trust or are already family members, friends or relations.

The sexual predator of today does not wear the obligatory 'dirty old mac'. Nor does he or she hide in alleyways or dark places. They seek their targets from a background of everyday occupations and walks of life, from the unemployed to highly respected members of many organisations.

Beneath the masks of everyday people, sexual predators will groom, coerce, manipulate, dominate, blackmail, tease, ridicule, finance, threaten or isolate in a cowardly and underhand manner in order to abuse, assault and psychologically disempower children, tearing away at their right to a childhood.

Before the abuse even takes place, the perpetrator will have threatened their target in one of the ways mentioned above into believing that not only might they be encouraging and causing the abuse to happen, but also that they won't be believed and/or harm will come to them or those they love in some way if they do tell.

Sexual abuse is the violation of a child, exposing or subjecting the child of either gender to sexual contact. It includes any type of abuse such as: oral, genital, anal, breast or buttock touching as well as using objects for penetration, sexual stimulation and exposure to sexualisation or fondling. Perpetrators of such behaviour can be male or female.

With so many high-profile names currently being called to account for historic sexual abuse against children, it begs the question: why now and why so many all at once? When the floodgates opened with the Jimmy Savile allegations, thousands of adults affected by childhood sexual violation watched closely, as those who felt safe enough to report the crimes that were committed against them were actually starting to be believed.

This instigated a situation in which many more adult victims of childhood sexual abuse sought validation, giving them the confidence to come forward with a clear and loud voice, to tell their own stories in the knowledge that now they might at least be listened to.Because of the recent disclosures across the United Kingdom, a new sense of hope has emerged for those who have yet to disclose their own experience with a possibility of finally being believed.

Any kind of sexual violation against another is a horrendous act borne of sexual deviance, of exerting power and control over a person less able to defend themselves, which leaves the abused person in a state of imbalance and emotional turmoil. When this type of abuse is perpetrated upon children, it is even more difficult for them to feel safe and manage their responses in an adult world.

Who are the victims?

Childhood sexual abuse can occur anywhere, in any population, race, culture or at any level of status. It happens to children in rural, towns and inner-city areas at all socio-economic and educational levels. Statistics indicate that while the majority of victims are girls, the number of boys is significantly increasing.

These are just *some*, but not all, existing common characteristics of backgrounds in which sexual abuse may occur:

- social isolation – victims of bullying

- care homes and 'invisible' children (lost in the system)

- domineering control-seeking parent

- absent or preoccupied mother (either physically or emotionally)

- having few boundaries

- having to assume a parental role at a young age.

Who are the perpetrators?

The most common perpetrators, committing the majority of sexual abuse, are people known to the child. This type of crime can occur within a family, the perpetrator being a parent, step-parent, guardian, older sibling or relative. It may be someone outside the family in a position of trust, such as family friend, dentist, doctor, teacher, police officer or other professional.

When researching a number of retrospective surveys on the internet, results have indicated that no more than 10 to 30 per cent of the offenders were strangers. Strangely enough, in 90 per cent of childhood sexual abuse cases in America, the offenders are male and are often described as being unassertive, withdrawn and emotionless.

Another common characteristic, but not always, is a history of abuse (this does not automatically mean that abuse will fire further abuse).

Perpetrators can be and are increasingly female. Women tend to use more persuasive measures, such as during bathing or applying creams, rather than force or threat of force, which are more common with male perpetrators and older, possibly teenage, victims.

Signs of abuse and long-term effects

Behavioural signs can be extreme changes; for example, a child who was always good at school and achieving top grades may suddenly become naughty and lose interest. Equally this may be reversed, as school can sometimes become a safe place of escape for a child subjected to sexual abuse at home. It is not uncommon for those who have suffered at the intrusive hands of an abuser as a child to be emotionally split off, being severely traumatised by the abuse on the one hand, but somehow managing to function and hold down a job, family and many other activities on the other. This is a coping mechanism and one that requires tremendous strength and courage. For the person who has been victimised, especially if they were initially disbelieved as a child, the details of the abuse will almost always be shameful, severe and distressing for the now adult, which alone may have prevented them from disclosing their ordeal to friends or family historically.

The abuse can affect every element of a child's developmental years and adult life, such as where they live, the partner/s they choose (if they are able to hold down a relationship at all), the clothes they wear, the job they do and ultimately the life they live.

Childhood targets of such abuse often experience a range of different symptomatic ailments and characteristic reactions as they become adults, and long after into their later years – here are just a few:

- eating disorders

- overly clinging/needy behaviour – in adults as well as children

- promiscuity – over-sexualised behaviour

- change in academic/work performance

- disturbed sleep patterns, affecting REM (rapid eye movement)

- illness and body reactions, especially those that involve the adrenal organs and systematic firing of the fight, flight or freeze mechanism

- problems with intimacy

- self-harm, for example cutting and blood letting

- depression and related symptoms

- phobias and obsessive compulsion disorders

- drug dependency – self-medication

- alcohol dependency – self-medication

- serial periods of homelessness

- suicide.

All of the above symptoms and many others may often be the adult survivor's direct attempt at either finding a way to control their lives, or finding a resource and outlet for their difficulties. As children who were often taught to keep secrets, those abused in childhood do not have the usual outlets – friends or family – so they have to find other ways to self-soothe. With this in mind, it makes sense for the surviving adult to act out in any of the above ways, if it brings solace of a kind, keeping them safe in their world.

When we look back to our childhood, we do so with our adult eyes and it can be easy to forget how vulnerable we were then. For an adult affected by childhood sexual abuse this can be even more difficult to comprehend.

Having someone trained to listen, not to apportion blame, judge or to give direction based on his or her own life, nor to give advice, just to be silent and allow a safe channel of disclosure for that persons' inner secret, can be an immeasurable sense of freedom for any adult affected by childhood sexual violation. It has been likened to taking off a very heavy backpack that has been carried since the abuse took place.

Sexual abuse by someone the person knows has the effect of making him or her feel less able to report the attack when that abuser, possibly a father, brother or well-loved uncle is responsible. This may be because they fear that they will not be believed, love the perpetrator or are simply just too terrified that the threats often promised will be followed through.

Sibling sexually abusive behaviours

Universally, siblings will know the wonder of having a loving, protective and close relationship with their brother or sister, both in their developing years and through to adulthood: watching each other's backs, sticking together, going through many of life's trials and tribulations from the births of their own children to the death of their parents, always supporting, always there for each other. This is society's expected scenario for siblings of both genders.

For some, however, it can be a very different picture; there are thousands of siblings who are systematically sexually abused by their brother/s and/or sister/s.

Incest is a taboo and a neglected social problem that has only started to receive significant attention in the United States in the last 30 years. Sibling sexual abuse has been identified as the most common form of incest; however, the origins and scope of incest are still not well understood and existing research literature is laden with definitional inconsistencies, data limitations, and inadequate research methodology. (DiClemente *et al.* 2015)

So, is it children abusing children or is it mutually consensual sexual exploration? In many situations either of these could be the case, however, when one sibling exerts his or her power, applied pressure or coercion over a younger sibling to submit to sexually inappropriate behaviours, it is then classed legally as sexually abusive behaviour.

Table 4.1 illustrates some of the differences between the three categories of sibling sexual behaviour as explored by Finkelhor (1980).

Table 4.1 Three main categories of sibling sexual interaction

SIBLING 'NORMAL' SEXUAL EXPLORATION ~ DEVELOPMENT

You show me yours and I'll show you mine. Playing doctors and nurses. Mummy and Daddy

Explorative behaviours considered part of normal development

Sexual interest often consensual and often with children of similar age

In 1980, a survey of 796 undergraduates, 15% of females and 10% males reported some form of sexual experience involving a sibling; most of these fell short of actual intercourse

A 1989 paper reported the results of a questionnaire with responses from 526 undergraduate college students in which 17% of the respondents stated that they had pre-adolescent sexual experiences with a sibling

Natural curiosity

Where do babies come from?

Noticing anatomical differences between males and females

Engagement in genital play or masturbation, exhibiting or inspecting genitals

SIBLING SEXUAL VIOLATION

Grooming

Coercion

Early sexualisation

Blaming/bullying

Pretend games leading to sexual activity

A quarter of the 1980 study stated that these experiences were described as abusive or exploitative

Excessive or public masturbation

Manipulating or tricking other children into non-consensual or inappropriate sexual activities – also referred to as 'child on child' sexual abuse

SIBLING SYSTEMATIC RAPE and ABUSE

Force by older brother or sister or both to have sexual intercourse against the will of the recipient

Regular/systematic incidents of rape and forced sexual activities

Power and control over a younger sibling

Older sibling/s being given responsibility of younger sibling/s therefore allowing power and control to take place and often to 'take hold' which can include:

Sexually gratifying behaviours

Possible introduction of friends to watch and/or take part in abuse of younger or more vulnerable siblings

Adapted from Finkelhor (1980)

The National Centre on Sexual Behaviour of Youth research has described infrequent and inappropriate sexual behaviours in children aged between two years and 12 years as shown in Table 4.2. The table lists sexual behaviours that are reported by parents of pre-school-age children to be infrequent or highly unusual. Some children who have been sexually abused display inappropriate sexual behaviours, and others have aggressive or highly problematic sexual behaviour. However, it should be noted that the majority of children who have been sexually abused do not have subsequent inappropriate or aggressive sexual behaviours.

Sibling abusive and/or incestuous interactions may take any of the forms shown in Figure 4.1. Variable and extensive internet research has shown studies do suggest that sibling/incest abuse, particularly of older brothers abusing younger siblings, is the most common form of incest abuse with some studies finding this type of abuse occurring more frequently than other forms.

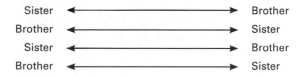

Figure 4.1 Forms of sibling abuse/incest

Some studies suggest that adolescent perpetrators of sibling abuse choose younger victims over a lengthier period and use violence more frequently and severely than adult perpetrators. It also suggests that sibling abuse has a higher rate of penetrative acts than father or stepfather incest, with father and older brother incest resulting in greater reported distress than stepfather abuse.

Hardly, if ever, is sibling sexual abuse mentioned in the press or by television media. In fact, it is swept under the carpet, possibly because of the confusion of the three main categories as Table 4.1 illustrates or because it is such an unreported crime. Time and again the safest space for such depth of disclosure is the confidentiality and safety of a therapy or other professional sessional room later in adulthood, and often this may be presented behind a different issue brought to therapy or support work.

The very mention of sibling sexual abuse and violation has the ability to strike a sense of distaste in most of us and is often passed off as 'boys will be boys' or 'children doing what children do'.

The primary element of sibling sexual abuse is having access to or responsibility for a younger sibling or siblings. Neglect and abuse perpetrated by parents creates a perfect environment for sibling sexual abuse to occur. Parents or caregivers who either disbelieve or accuse their children of constantly telling lies compound the situation. They, in fact, further perpetrate the sibling abuse by secondary injury, leaving the child in a helpless state, believing that there is no way out.

The effects of sibling sexual abuse

For us as adults to thrive and prosper, we need to have choices in our lives. We can choose to build our own prisons for which we always hold the key, emotionally, physically, financially or in the commitments we make to others. When any form of sexual abuse takes place in childhood, the effects can limit choices later in life, as the confidence in those who are expected to trust and care for us slowly ebbs away. This can and often does result in a person's foundation and structure becoming completely undermined and unstable, as if the abuser eternally holds the key.

What makes this worse is that when childhood sexual abuse is perpetrated by a sibling, it's a secret too dark, too distressing and too shameful to contemplate exposing, which is why it's often disclosed much later on in life, if at all.

Unfortunately not all adults affected by childhood sibling sexual abuse have much support later in life and the consequences of such trauma can manifest in many different ways. As well as all the other consequences, the ultimate cost is the devastating effects it often has within adult intimate relationships.

The effects of sexual abuse in childhood, whether the perpetrator is a parent, sibling, aunt, uncle, extended family member, neighbour, a friend of the family or a complete stranger, are devastatingly shocking to the person affected. Any sexual violation of a childhood can be like a fiery dart, stinging, wounding and leaving the child with extreme unspent emotion – unspent because childhood victims do not have the capacity to externalise their pain and do so by turning in on their self (inward). Shutting down is a child's normal response mechanism to danger in order to keep safe and survive.

Sibling abuse can be one of the most difficult to understand, not least because of an unconditional love element. The victim often complies in order to maintain this love.

From the many victims of sibling sexual abuse who have shared their childhood journey through our therapy rooms the evaluations have evidenced that the most common consequence in adulthood is that of a sense of loss: loss of childhood, loss of a potential sibling relationship and layer upon layer of regret, shame, injustice, trust issues, betrayal and an ingrained inability to maintain intimate relationships.

On reflection, many adults will state that the abuse they suffered as children at the hands of their siblings has left them scarred with what they believe is irreparable damage. This work can often be extremely complex for the client to process.

When parents or siblings use their younger family members to gratify themselves by sexually exerting power and control, it is like life for the young person stands still and they are floating, walking through an unreal invisible journey of blackened tar, every corner of life shrouded in silence, secrecy and shame. This ranges from the blatant crossing of a child's sexual boundary by mothers, sisters and female relations, often veiled under age-inappropriate bathing and medical application regimes, to constant humiliation, psychological and bullying behaviours from fathers, brothers and uncles passing their daughters, sons, sisters and nieces to each other like broken rag dolls.

One might be forgiven for thinking that a person who has endured such profound trauma may never get over it. The good news is that with the right help and the right intervention for healing and recovery, people do recover from the perverse acts that others perpetrate upon them, and they are able to maintain good healthy futures.

Table 4.2 Infrequent and inappropriate sexual behaviours aged 2–12 years

Puts mouth on sex parts	Asks to engage in sex acts
Puts objects in rectum or vagina	Imitates sexual intercourse
Masturbates with objects	Undresses other people
Touches other's sex parts after being told not to	Asks to watch sexually explicit television
Touches adults sex parts	Makes sexual sounds

(Adapted from Silovsky and Bonner 2003)

Grooming and conditioning behaviours

Grooming is continuous within many childhood and adolescent years. Sexual predators use their own form of grooming and conditioning to coerce children in order to feed their depraved sexual fantasies and to overpower their prey in order to exert systematic control and sexual abuse.

Grooming and/or conditioning is the way in which a sexual predator whose modus operandi (MO, the term used by law enforcement authorities to describe the particular manner in which a crime is committed) is the sexual exploitation of children of either gender. It is the slow manipulative process in which a paedophile (an adult who is sexually interested in children) or sexual predator will creep his/her way in to be around his/her victim/s' lives. All known factors contributing to child sexual abuse can be grouped into preconditions (see Table 4.3). These are:

- *Motivation:* The potential abuser needs to have some motivation to sexually abuse a child/children. Thus he/she will need to find children erotically and sexually desirable.

- *Internal inhibitors:* The potential abuser must overcome internal inhibitors that may act against his/her motivation to sexually abuse.

- *External inhibitors:* The potential abuser also has to overcome external obstacles and inhibitions prior to sexually abusing a child/children.

- *Resistance:* Finally, the potential abuser has to overcome the child's possible resistance to being sexually abused.

Table 4.3 Preconditions to child sexual abuse

Precondition 1: Factors related to motivation to abuse

Emotional congruence	Arrested emotional development. Need to feel powerful and controlling. Re-enactment of childhood trauma to undo the hurt. Narcissistic identification with self as a young child.	Masculine requirement to be dominant and powerful in sexual relationship.
Sexual arousal	Childhood sexual experience that was traumatic or strongly conditioning. Modelling of sexual interest in children by someone else. Biological abnormality.	Child pornography. Erotic portrayal of children in advertising. Male tendency to sexualise all emotional needs
Blockage	Oedipal conflict. Castration anxiety. Fear of adult females. Traumatic sexual experience with adult. Inadequate social skills. Marital problems	Repressive norms about masturbation and extra marital sex.

Precondition 2: Factors predisposing to overcoming internal inhibitors to abuse

	Alcohol, psychosis, impulse disorder, senility.Failure of incest inhibition mechanism in the family dynamics.	Social tolerance of sexual interest in children. Weak criminal sanctions against offenders. Social tolerance for offences committed while intoxicated. Male inability to identify with needs of children.

Precondition 3: Factors predisposing to overcoming external inhibitors to abuse

	Mother who is absent (either physically or emotionally) or ill. Mother who is not close to or protective of child. Mother who is dominated or abused by father. Social isolation of family. Lack of supervision of child. Unusual sleeping or bedroom conditions.	Lack of social supports for barriers to women's equality. Erosion of social networks. Ideology of family sanctity.

Precondition 4: Factors predisposing to overcoming child's resistance

	Child who is emotionally insecure or deprived. Child who lacks knowledge about sexual abuse. Situation of unusual trust between child and perpetrator	Unavailability of sex education for children. Social powerlessness of children

(Adapted from Finkelhor 1984)   **59**

Grooming and conditioning in order to sexually abuse a child or children more commonly takes place at the hands of a familiar face, rather than the stranger or 'monster' in the park.

Nowadays children are not allowed 'free run' as they were or 'to play in the streets', so paedophiles have to be more manipulative in their search for the right target. Although we do sometimes hear of prowling sexual predators in alleyways and walkways, watching schools and covertly taking photographs of children, they are usually taken care of very quickly.

The law is set out to protect the photographing of children without parents' or guardians' consent as in the Sex Offences Act 2003. Almost anyone who sees a stranger outside organisations such as schools, swimming baths and ice skating rinks will report them and the offences that cover these situations can be found in the Children's Act 1978.

Grooming behaviour includes psychological, physical and emotional manipulation of a child or young person and also the steady grooming of those closely connected to that child to gain their trust. The trusting relationship within a family means that they are often less likely to believe accusations.

The panic in society caused by some high profile cases such as the murder of James Bulger in 1993 and the abductions of Madeleine McCann in 2007 and Shannon Matthews in 2008, to mention just a few, has amplified fear for children's safety among parents and those caring for children.

Such cases are, even now, quite rare compared to the number of children affected and victimised by child sexual abuse by people that are known to them, including members of their own family. It is crucial that children are taught the dangers of going anywhere at all with strangers but more importantly to teach the dangers of strange behaviour in adults especially in those that they know, including family members.

There is now a campaign developed by the National Society for the Prevention of Cruelty to Children (NSPCC) that gives a clear message to parents to work through with their children.[1]

The following are common grooming behaviours of sexual predators:

- *Finding excuses to be around children:* Putting themselves in touch with children, either through schools, within families, babysitting, out of school clubs, the voluntary sector, as well as vulnerable children in care, hospitals and similar situations.

- *Building trust with children and those responsible:* Forging relationships at every level with main caregivers. This could also be other parents who prey on children outside their own families.

- *Buying gifts and sweets:* Providing trendy clothes, jewellery, sweets and the latest fashionable gear, mobile phones, iPads and so on.

- *Building a 'special' friendship by providing a place of empathy:* Allowing the child/adolescent to talk about any problems that they may be having within their family, therefore feeding the sexual predator with ammunition for later, should he/she need it for a blackmail scenario.

- *Keeping secrets:* Teaching the child to tell lies or just not tell others about their 'special friendship', because if they did, they would not be allowed to be friends any more.

- *Making up touching games:* An arm around the shoulder or hug to comfort the victim, increasing over time to other touching behaviours.

- *Blaming the child or young person for the abuse:* Because earlier on the child may have been okay with the odd arm around the shoulder, the sexual predator may then blame the child

---

1   This campaign and printed brochure can easily be downloaded by following this link: www.nspcc.org.uk/underwearrule

for leading him/her on when the touching increases further, leading to self-blame, therefore causing of the abuse.

- *Threats to harm other family members:* Telling the child that if he or she tells anyone about the sexually abusive part of their relationship, they will kill or harm a sibling or other family member or that he or she won't be believed or will be taken away to another family.

- *Voyeurism:* Watching children, secretly spying on them for sexual gratification.

- *Frottage:* Rubbing up against children for sexual gratification, such as doormen/women in children's youth clubs and discos.

- *Exhibitionism:* Indecently exposing sexual parts of self in order to groom and get children 'used to' seeing genitalia, thus normalising exposure.

- *Pornography:* Forcing or coercing children to watch pornographic videos, YouTube footage and DVDs and look at magazines in order to sexualise them for further sexual abuse.

Section 15 of the Sex Offences Act 2003 lays out the guidelines of grooming in a concise way; the section that follows is given in its original form to illustrate the law:

Culpability and harm

The sentences for public protection must be considered in all cases. They are designed to ensure that sexual offenders are not released into the community if they present a significant risk of serious harm. In a case where no substantive sexual offence has in fact been committed, the main dimension of seriousness will be the offender's intention – the more serious the offence intended, the higher the offender's culpability. The harm to the victim in such cases will invariably be less than that resulting from a completed offence, although the risk to which the victim has been put is always a relevant factor. In some cases, where the offender has come quite close to fulfilling his or her intention, the victim may have been put in considerable fear, and psychological and physical injury to the victim is a possible feature. In addition to the generic aggravating factors identified in the guidelines on seriousness, the main factors determining the seriousness of a preparatory offence are:

- the seriousness of the intended offence (which will affect both the offender's culpability and the degree of risk to which the victim has been exposed)

- the degree to which the offence was planned

- the sophistication of the grooming

- the determination of the offender

- how close the offender came to success

- the reason why the offender did not succeed, i.e. whether it was a change of mind or whether someone or something prevented the offender from continuing

- any physical or psychological injury suffered by the victim.

The starting point should be proportionate with that for the preparatory offence actually committed, with an enhancement to reflect the nature and severity of the intended sexual offence.

Sarah's Law: Child Sex Offenders Disclosure Scheme

Since April 2011, those who pose a risk to children are able to be identified by parents, guardians and those caring for children by using the Government's Child Sex Offenders Disclosure Scheme, also referred to as Sarah's Law.

This excellent scheme allows for enquiry into whether a person who has access to a child is a registered sex offender or poses a risk to that child. All cases are dealt with individually and in isolation, and any disclosure will only be made to protective and/or safeguarding adults.[2]

---

2   For practitioner guidance and tools to help practitioners implement the sex offender disclosure scheme, see www.gov.uk/goverment/publications/child-sex-offender-disclosure-scheme-guidance

5

Internet Child Pornography and Pseudo Paedophilia

The different faces of the internet

The internet, full of knowledge and inspiration, is an international doorway to unknown territory. For most of us it is a daily and continuous source of communication, information and learning. It is possible to purchase just about anything without leaving the house; items of desire can be delivered to our door within a couple of days. Unfortunately, this convenient invention also brings with it a darker and more sinister side, arming paedophiles and sexual deviants who prey on children and adolescents with the opportunity to groom and entice them unsuspectingly into dangerous situations.

For a full and complete look at the Sex Offences Act you can dowlnload the PDF version. However, for the purposes of this chapter, I cite two sections (15 and 24), of the Sexual Offences Act 2003 in order to provide an understanding of which activities are breaches and are punishable by law.

15. An offence under section 160 of the Criminal Justice Act 1988 (c. 33) (possession of indecent photograph of a child), if the indecent photographs or pseudo-photographs showed persons under 16 and—

> (a) the conviction, finding or caution was before the commencement of this Part, or

(b) the offender—

  (i) was 18 or over, or

  (ii) is sentenced in respect of the offence to imprisonment for a term of at least 12 months.

24. An offence under section 15 of this Act (meeting a child following sexual grooming etc.).

Now that access to the internet has become as available as a daily newspaper, finding child pornography is much easier and more worldwide than ever before.

Pornography is a huge facet of the internet and comes in all manner of formats, a mixture of erotic text, audio stories, video clips, YouTube footage, photographs, sex chat, live feeds and so on. Anything from straight sex to fetish and specialty pornography can be found, if the user knows where to look.

To consenting adults, this way of life is about choice, and most of the above is legal; exceptions to this are: child pornography, extreme sado-masochism, bestiality and necrophilia.

In July 2013 Prime Minister David Cameron first made a speech about making it difficult to access pornography on the internet. The National Society for the Prevention of Cruelty to Children (NSPCC) hosted his speech. A year later he began the parliamentary 2014 summer recess with a speech outlining ways in which the government will clamp down on internet pornography.[1]

A child who is feeling lonely, bullied or isolated from their family or friends for a multitude of reasons would welcome an email, text message, WhatsApp, Snapchat or similar such as:

---

1   To see the full version you can follow this link: www.gov.uk/government/speeches/the-internet-and-pornography-prime-minister-calls-for-action

> I know your loneliness, I can be your friend and you will never be lonely again

> Olds shout when we smoke, we all smoke – I understand wot it's like it's not yr fault. U need to get outa there...

> We can always be friends, those girls are just jealous...let's meet up at the park today

> You don't need to worry about your Mum she's mad. Just stay friends with me, we can share our secrets and one day we can run away from them all

> My Mum is always hitting me as well, especially when she's been drinking – will you just keep talking to me

Hundreds of thousands of messages like these are found on the walls and inboxes of social networking sites of children and young people who believe that they are from individuals of their own age group.

Once an empty space in the child's life has been targeted and filled, the sexual predator can then continue to form deeper emotional bonds and the child can eventually be groomed successfully towards meeting up.

Pseudo paedophilia

Sophisticated technology and internet security presents a major challenge to the enforcement agencies which leaves child-based pornographic websites, forums and community groups free to continually provide and circulate child pornography and abusive images.

Pseudo-photographs are images which appear to be photographs made by computer graphics. The good news is that as fast as paedophiles can create grooming situations and internet exchanges of child images, law enforcement worldwide is continually in operation to locate evidence and convict the sexual predators of children. As technology updates allowing paedophiles to find new ways to access children so too does the capability of those chasing them.

1. Indecent photographs of children.

1. It is an offence for a person:

    (a) to take, or permit to be taken [F1or to make], any indecent photograph [F1or pseudo-photograph]of a child F2...; or

    (b) to distribute or show such indecent photographs [F3or pseudo-photographs]; or

    (c) to have in his possession such indecent photographs [F3or pseudo-photographs], with a view to their being distributed or shown by himself or others; or

    (d) to publish or cause to be published any advertisement likely to be understood as conveying that the advertiser distributes or shows such indecent photographs [F3or pseudo-photographs], or intends to do so.

2. For purposes of this Act, a person is to be regarded as distributing an indecent photograph [F4or pseudo-photograph]if he parts with possession of it to, or exposes or offers it for acquisition by, another person.

3. Proceedings for an offence under this Act shall not be instituted except by or with the consent of the Director of Public Prosecutions.

4. Where a person is charged with an offence under subsection (1) (b) or (c), it shall be a defence for him to prove.

    (a) that he had a legitimate reason for distributing or showing the photographs [F5or pseudo-photographs] or (as the case may be) having them in his possession; or

    (b) that he had not himself seen the photographs [F5or pseudo-photographs]and did not know, nor had any cause to suspect, them to be indecent.

5. References in the M1Children and Young Persons Act 1933 (except in sections 15 and 99) to the offences mentioned in Schedule 1 to that Act shall include an offence under subsection (1)(a) above.

6. .... F6

7. In paragraph 1 of the Schedule of Visiting Forces Act 1952 (offences against the person in the case of which a member of a visiting force is in certain circumstances not liable to be tried by a United Kingdom court), after sub-paragraph (b)(viii) (inserted by the Sexual Offences Act 1956) there shall be added— "(ix) section 1(1)(a) of the Protection of Children Act 1978".

Civic Government (Scotland) Act 1982-Section 52

The 'making' offence

Causing an indecent photograph of a child to exist on a computer screen is considered to be 'making an indecent photograph of a child'. A person who either downloads images on to disc or who prints them off is making them. The Act is not only concerned with the original creation of images, but also their proliferation.

'Photographs or pseudo-photographs found on the internet may have originated from outside the United Kingdom; to download or print within the jurisdiction is to create new material which hitherto may not have existed therein.' (R v Bowden (1999)).

The Sexual Offences Act 2003 further amended the 1978 Act so as to increase the age of a child from 16 to 18. The 2003 Act also added a defence to cover the situation where an 'indecent photograph of a child' was created by that child's partner. Because of the Bowden decision, it was also necessary to add a defence where it was necessary to make an indecent photograph or pseudo-photograph for the purposes of a criminal investigation.

1. **Subject to sections 1A and 1B**, it is an offence for a person–

(a) to take, or permit to be taken or to make, any indecent photograph or pseudo-photograph of a child; or

(b) to distribute or show such indecent photographs or pseudo-photographs; or

(c) to have in his possession such indecent photographs or pseudo-photographs, with a view to their being distributed or shown by himself or others; or

(d) to publish or cause to be published any advertisement likely to be understood as conveying that the advertiser distributes or shows such indecent photographs or pseudo-photographs or intends to do so.

Definition of photograph

'Photograph' shall include film, video-recording, copy of photograph or film or video, recording, photo comprised in a film or video-recording; negatives of photograph etc.; data on a computer etc. which can be converted to photograph etc.[1]

Definition of indecent

The Act does not define the term 'indecent'.[1]

Definition of pseudo-photograph

The Act defines a 'pseudo-photograph' as 'an image, whether made by computer-graphics or otherwise howsoever, which appears to be a photograph', and further a copy of a pseudo-photograph, including data stored on a computer disc or by any other form of electronic means that can be converted into a pseudo- photograph.[1][2]

---

2   www.legislation.gov.uk/ukpga/1978/37/body

6

Child Sex Trafficking and Prostitution

Child trafficking is one form of the illegal trade of human beings for the purpose, among others, of child and adult prostitution. Children in this arena are continuously at the hands of the adults who exploit, procure and abuse their bodies leaving them emotionally scarred and physically numb well into adulthood. The reasons for trafficking are very diverse. They include: fragile socio-economic conditions; vulnerable family environments; lack of awareness towards children, including lack of birth registration; armed conflicts and natural disasters; the HIV/AIDS epidemic; and gender/minority discrimination.

Child trafficking is one form of the illegal trade of human beings for the purpose, among others, of child and adult prostitution. Children in this arena are continuously at the hands of the adults who exploit, procure and abuse their bodies leaving them emotionally scarred and physically numb well into adulthood. The reasons for trafficking are very diverse. They include: fragile socio-economic conditions; vulnerable family environments; lack of awareness and care towards children, including lack of birth registration; armed conflicts and natural disasters; the HIV/AIDS epidemic; and gender/minority discrimination.

British national children or young people can also be victims of trafficking within the UK. This occurs when the victims are moved from one location to another irrespective of distance. This may be within a town or between towns in the UK, very often for the purposes of sexual exploitation.

This 'internal trafficking' is not limited to girls and young women; young boys and men can also be targets. As migration opportunities increase by way of work and access to different countries, this widens the opening for the crime of human trafficking. There are regular news reports of more and more children who are lost and alone in the most appalling conditions at the hands of sexual predators.

More and more, the media covers these unspeakable stories of human trafficking and child exploitation. The traffickers exploit vulnerable and poverty stricken families with promises of work and a new life for their children. Just like those who groom children for sex, these perpetrators lie, cheat and con their way in to the hearts of parents in order to get their needs met.

Case Study

Gabija was 22 when she came to therapy to work through her relationship issues. From Lithuania she spoke excellent English. On completing her initial assessment, Gabija related to me that her childhood was beautiful until she reached 11 years old.

She recalled that the day after her eleventh birthday: two men came to their house and spoke with her parents, while she was sent to her room. They ate and drank, and later that evening her mother told her that these men would return the next day to take her on an exciting adventure to Europe where she could learn and pave the way for her family to join her later. Gabi, as she was known to her family, remembered that she was very frightened but excited at the same time.

Gabi recollected the journey. She'd been taken on board a huge boat and as she spoke gently, her physical reaction demonstrated the deep-seated trauma that she was holding within her: her hands started to shake, the skin on her neck reddened, her breathing quickened and she developed a glazed look as she spoke about the boat where she'd been made to hide under some boxes in the hold.

Arriving in the United Kingdom at a place her young mind couldn't take in because of its vastness and the number of people, which was in fact the terminal at Folkestone. She was quickly ushered out of the boat with two other young girls of around the same age and put into a shiny black car. It was a very long drive; she remembered feeling sick and tired. Gabi and three other girls were taken to a house on a large housing estate in Leeds and there they were given food and a drink, shown to the bathroom and given some fresh clothing.

For three days the four young girls were kept in this house while one woman and two men, who they couldn't understand, kept watch and made them try new clothes and put on make-up.

From there on, she was forced into a life of child prostitution from a bigger house, also in Leeds, and she recalled being terrified every minute of every day. She stated that somehow, something inside her stopped her from taking the drugs that so many of the other girls took to 'get them through', and when she was 17 she got away.

There was one day, she said, that was like no other. She had eight hundred pounds on her that she was supposed to give in to the men who 'owned' her. As she spoke about that day her body tensed up as she recalled the moment that she literally walked out of a house where everyone was asleep, she got on a bus and then a train, ending up in a completely new city. She had enough money to stay in a bed and breakfast while she found work in a restaurant kitchen. She changed the colour of her hair, her identity and started a new life. She met a fellow Lithuanian man called Lukas and they set up home together. Her life when she came into therapy was very different from the life she had described at the initial assessment session.

On reflection she had decided that however she had got to Europe she was glad she had; her parents had even managed to come and visit and to meet their grandson. We worked with a Trauma Tapestry, Gabi was good at art and this was the way she felt that she wanted to work. She was able to find release and stated that with every new drawing she felt she had released more of the toxic core within her, which in turn helped with her relationship issues.

Human trafficking for slavery and/or sexual violence is not a new criminal activity, it has been with us for many years as Gabija's story demonstrates.

The Home Office produces a frontline staff guidance publication, which gives comprehensive information about every aspect of human trafficking.[1]

For up to date statistics on the human trafficking illegal trade you can visit Stop the Traffic.[2]

Organisations such as Unseen[3] work tirelessly to provide services for those who have survived modern day slavery and exploitation. They accept referrals from all over the UK and are an excellent resource for signposting clients who are survivors of the slave and human trafficking illegal trade.

For additional information you can keep up to date with the Child Exploitation and Online Protection (Ceop) Centre Strategic Threat Assessment and the Department of Health (DoH) Safeguarding Children Involved in Prostitution Supplementary Guidance to Working Together to Safeguard Children. www.ceop.police.[4]

Her eyes tell the story – of a thousand dark days
Caught in greed – of grown up ways
Give her strength to be free – love to be sure
Those men outside – won't hurt her anymore
Let's protect our children – in every way
Giving them courage – for a brand new day

Sue Daniels

---

1   www.gov.uk/government/uploads/system/uploads/attachment_data/file/509326/victims-of-modern-slavery-frontline-staff-guidance-v3.pdf

2   www.stopthetraffik.org/spot/statistics

3   www.unseenuk.org/

4   uk/Documents/ceopdocs/Child_Trafficking_Strategic_Threat_Assessment_2010_NPM_Final.pdf

7

Sexually Transmitted Infections (STIs)

When a person has been raped, there are many consequences for them to bear in the aftermath. One of the most traumatic can be contracting either a sexually transmitted disease and, if female, becoming pregnant, or both. In this chapter, I give an outline of the most common sexually transmitted diseases and their treatments.

Gonorrhea

What is it? Gonorrhea is a sexually transmitted infection (which used to be known as 'the clap'). It is caused by a bacterium called Neisseria gonorrhea or gonococcus. The bacteria are found mainly in the semen of infected men and vaginal fluids of infected women, so gonorrhea is easily passed between people through sexual contact.

How is it spread? Having unprotected sex – including oral and anal sex – and sharing vibrators or other sex toys which have not been washed or covered with a new condom. Gonorrhea is the second most common sexually transmitted infection in the UK with over 19,000 cases reported in 2006. Young men aged 20–24 years and women aged 16–19 are most commonly affected.

Symptoms   Symptoms of gonorrhea usually show up one to 14 days after infection. However, symptoms may not appear until many months later, or not until the infection has spread to other parts of the body. About 50 per cent of women and 10 per cent of men who have contracted gonorrhea do not experience any symptoms when they are infected, which means it can often go untreated for some time.

For women
- a strong, unpleasant smelling thick discharge from the vagina, which may appear green or yellow in colour

- pain or tenderness in the lower abdominal area, including a burning sensation when urinating and a frequent need to urinate

- irritation or discharge from the anus

- bleeding between periods or heavier periods.

For men
- a thick white, yellow or green-coloured discharge from the tip of the penis

- pain or tenderness caused by inflammation of the testicles or prostate gland

- pain or burning sensation when urinating.

About 90 per cent of men who contract gonorrhea experience symptoms after they are infected.

Treatment   Gonorrhea is treated with a single dose of antibiotics, usually ceftriaxone, cefiximine or spectinomycin. The antibiotics are either given orally (a pill) or through an injection.

Genital warts

What is it?
Genital warts are small fleshy growths, which may appear anywhere on a man or woman's genital area. A virus called human papilloma virus (HPV) causes them. There are more than 60 different types of HPV. Some types cause warts to grow on the genitals; others cause warts to grow on different parts of the body, such as the hands.

How is it spread?
Warts are spread through skin-to-skin contact. They can be passed on during vaginal or anal sex.

Symptoms
After infection with a wart virus it usually takes between one and three months for warts to appear on the genitals. They may appear as pinkish/white small lumps or larger cauliflower-shaped lumps on the genital area. Warts can appear around the vulva, the penis, the scrotum or the anus. They may appear singularly or in groups. They may itch but are usually painless.

For women
A few types of the wart virus are linked to changes in cervical cells, which could eventually lead to cervical cancer. These changes can take many years, so it is important that every sexually active woman has regular cervical smear tests, whether or not she has genital warts. Cervical smear tests pick up these changes, before they become cancerous.

For men
There is no evidence to suggest that the wart virus may be linked to cancer in men at this time.

Treatment The aims of the treatment are to remove visible genital warts and reduce the amount of the virus, which should help the body to fight the infection. As a virus and not bacteria causes genital warts, antibiotics will not get rid of them. Visible warts can be removed by:

- putting cream or liquid onto the warts (this can be done at home or at the clinic)

- freezing (cryotherapy) or heat (electrocautery) surgery

- laser treatment

- injecting a drug directly into the wart, although this treatment is less common.

These treatments may be uncomfortable but they should not be painful. Sometimes a local anaesthetic cream is used. Treatments can cause irritation and soreness for a couple of days, so the doctor may prescribe painkillers.

Chlamydia

What is it? Chlamydia is one of the most common STIs. If left untreated, it can cause painful complications and serious health problems such as infertility. Chlamydia is a bacterium, which is found in the semen and vaginal fluids of men and women who have the infection. It is easily passed from one person to another through sexual contact.

How is it spread? Chlamydia is usually passed from one person to another during sex. Infection can be passed if in contact with semen or vaginal fluids of an individual who already has the infection. It is most commonly spread by having unprotected vaginal, anal or oral sex and sharing sex toys.

Symptoms   About 70–80 per cent of infected men and women will not have any obvious signs or symptoms, or they may be so mild that they are not noticed. Signs and symptoms can show up one to three weeks after coming into contact with Chlamydia, many months later, or not until the infection spreads to other parts of the body.

For women
- bleeding between periods and/or heavier periods (including women who are using hormonal contraception)

- bleeding after sex

- pain and/or bleeding when the woman has sex

- lower abdominal pain (pelvic pain)

- an unusual vaginal discharge

- pain when passing urine.

The antibiotics that are used to treat Chlamydia interact with the combined contraceptive pill and the contraceptive patch.

For men
- a white/cloudy or watery discharge from the tip of the penis

- pain when passing urine

- painful swelling of the testicles.

Treatment   The common treatment for Chlamydia is a course of antibiotics, which, if taken according to the instructions, is at least 95 per cent effective. Early treatment involves taking a course of antibiotic tablets either as a single dose or a longer course (up to two weeks). If there is a high chance of having contracted the infection, treatment can be started before the results of the tests are back. Partners are always given treatment as well. Other treatment may be needed if complications have occurred.

Trichomonas Vaginalis (TV)

What is it?	This STI is caused by a tiny parasite. This produces an infection in the vagina and sometimes in the urethra in men. It is usually sexually transmitted.
How is it spread?	Sexual transmission is via penetrative sex with someone who has the infection. Sharing moist towels, wash cloths, jacuzzis or hot baths where the parasite can live can also result in infection, although becoming infected via these non-sexual routes is extremely rare.
Symptoms	Up to 50 per cent of infected people will not have any symptoms at all. Symptoms can show up three to 21 days after coming into contact with trichomonas.

For women

• a change in vaginal discharge; this may increase, become thinner, frothy, or change in colour and develop a musty or fishy smell

• soreness, inflammation and itching in and around the vagina

• pain when passing urine

• pain when having sex

• lower abdominal tenderness.

For men

• a discharge from the penis, which may be thin and whitish

• pain or burning sensation when passing urine

• inflammation of the glands and foreskin (this is uncommon).

Treatment   Treatment of trichomonas is simple and involves taking antibiotics. There are several different antibiotics that can be used. These are taken either as a single dose or a longer course (up to one week). If there is a high chance of having contracted the infection especially due to a sexual assault, treatment can be started before the test results are back.

Syphilis

What is it?   Syphilis is a sexually transmitted infection. It has been relatively rare in the UK for several decades, but recent trends show that more people are becoming infected. If left untreated it can cause serious health problems in both men and women.

How is it spread?   Syphilis is spread from one person to another during sexual activity and by skin-to-skin contact with someone who has syphilis sores or rashes. Once the infection is in the body it can remain and be passed on before symptoms are noticeable, or after they've disappeared. Syphilis can be transmitted by blood transfusion, but all UK donors are screened to prevent this. It is also possible for a woman to pass the infection to her unborn baby.

Symptoms   *First stage:*

One or more sores – usually painless – will appear where bacteria entered the body. On average this will be three to four weeks after coming into contact with syphilis but could be longer. These sores can appear anywhere on the body. The symptoms are the same for both men and women. They can be difficult to recognise and can be missed.

Second stage:

If the infection remains untreated the second stage usually occurs some weeks after the appearance of sores. The symptoms include:

- a painless rash – not normally itchy – spreading all over the body, or in patches, often including the palms of the hands and soles of the feet

- flat, warty-looking growths in the vulva in women and around the anus in both men and women

- a flu-like illness, tiredness and loss of appetite, with swollen glands, which can last for weeks or months

- white patches on the tongue or roof of the mouth

- patchy hair loss.

This second stage of syphilis is very infectious and may last several weeks or months.

Third stage:

This is also known as the Latent Stage. When the infection remains untreated, it is called latent syphilis and can still be infectious. During this stage, the person infected may have no further symptoms. A latent period with no symptoms or obvious signs can last a lifetime. If left untreated, syphilis may start to cause very serious damage to the heart, brain, eyes, other internal organs, bones and nervous system and this can prove fatal.

For women	In women, the sores appear mainly on the vulva, the clitoris, cervix, around the opening of the urethra and around the anus.
For men	In men, they appear mainly around the opening of the urethra, on the penis and foreskin and around the anus and mouth.
Treatment	Treatment of first and second stage syphilis is simple and involves having just a single antibiotic injection or a course of injections or taking antibiotic tablets or capsules.

Pubic lice

This is not classed as an STI but can be contracted via sexual assault.

What are they?	Pubic lice are tiny parasitic insects that live in coarse body hair, such as pubic hair. They are yellow grey and about 2mm long. They have a crab like appearance, so they are often known as 'crabs'. Nits are the eggs, which appear as brownish dots fixed to the hair.
How are they spread?	Pubic lice are easily passed from one person to another through close body or sexual contact. They can be found in pubic hair, underarm and leg hair, the abdomen and chest, eyelashes and occasionally in eyebrows and beards. They do not live in hair on the head. The lice move by crawling from hair to hair, they cannot fly or jump.

Symptoms   Some people will not notice any symptoms, or may not notice the lice or eggs.

It can take several weeks after coming into contact with pubic lice before signs and symptoms may appear which are the same for both men and women:

- itching in the affected area/s

- black powdery droppings from the lice in undergarments

- brown eggs on pubic or other body hair

- irritation and inflammation in the affected area, sometimes caused by scratching

- sky-blue spots (which disappear within a few days) or very tiny specks of blood on the skin.

Treatment   Treatment for pubic lice is simple and involves using a special cream, lotion or shampoo. There are several different types that can be used. Cream, lotion or shampoo is applied to the affected areas. Some treatments can be rinsed off after fifteen minutes; others are left on for two, twelve or twenty-four hours. Some treatments need to be repeated after three to seven days.

Scabies

This is not classed as an STI but can be contracted via sexual assault.

What is it?

Tiny parasitic mites cause scabies. About 0.4mm long, smaller than a pinhead, they burrow into the skin and lay eggs. A more severe and uncommon form of the condition occurs when there are very many mites in the skin. This is called crusted scabies, and can affect older people and people with certain illnesses such as HIV.

How is it spread?

Scabies is easily passed from one person to another through close body or sexual contact with someone who has scabies. Both men and women can get scabies and pass it on. The mites which cause scabies can be found in the genital area, on the hands, between the fingers, on the wrists and elbows, underneath the arms, on the abdomen, on the breasts, around the nipple in women, on the feet and ankles and around the buttocks.

The mites can live for up to 72 hours off the body, so occasionally it is possible for scabies to be spread by clothing, bedding and towels.

Symptoms

It can take up to six weeks after coming into contact with scabies before signs and symptoms may appear. These are the same for both men and women as follows:

- intense itching in the affected areas, which may only be noticed at night or becomes worse in bed or after a hot bath or shower

- an itchy rash or tiny spots

- inflammation or raw, broken skin in the affected areas, usually caused by scratching.

Treatment Treatment for scabies is simple and involves using a special cream or lotion. There are several different types that can be used. Cream or lotion is usually applied to the whole body. Some treatments can be rinsed off after eight hours others are left on for 12 or 24 hours. Some treatments need to be repeated once after seven days, others are used for three days in a row.

Hepatitis B (HBV)

What is it? An inflammation of the liver. This can be caused by alcohol and some drugs, but usually it is the result of a viral infection. There are many types of virus, which can cause hepatitis. Each of these acts differently.

How is it spread? The virus can be spread in the following ways:

- by unprotected penetrative sex (when the penis enters the vagina, anus or mouth) with someone who is infected

- by sex which draws blood with someone who is infected by sharing contaminated needles or other drug-injecting equipment

- by using non-sterilised equipment for tattooing, acupuncture or body piercing

- from an infected mother to her baby, mainly during delivery (immunisation of the baby at birth prevents the transmission of Hep B)

- through a blood transfusion where blood is not tested for the Hep B virus (all blood for transfusion in the UK is tested).

Symptoms   People may have no symptoms at all, but the virus can still be passed on to others. Symptoms are the same for men and women and may include:

- a short mild flu-like illness

- nausea and vomiting

- diarrhea

- loss of appetite

- weight loss

- jaundice (yellow skin and whites of eyes, darker yellow urine and pale faeces)

- itchy skin.

Treatment   Many people do not need treatment, as the inflammation of the liver may not be severe. If treatment is needed for liver inflammation, a referral to a specialist centre for a full assessment will be required. Treatments for HBV include drugs such as Interferon that work on the immune system.

Recently, other drugs such as Lamivudine and Famciclovir have been investigated for this purpose. For HBV carriers co-infected with HIV they may be more infectious; however, the inflammatory activity in the liver may actually be reduced, as their immune system will be impaired.

Genital Herpes (HSV)

What is it?   Genital herpes is a common STI – a virus called herpes simplex, which can spread during vaginal, anal or oral sex or by sharing sex toys. The condition may be painful and stressful. An outbreak or attack of genital herpes is usually called an episode.

How is it spread?

Genital herpes is spread from one person to another during sexual contact where one is having an outbreak of genital herpes at the time or by skin-to-skin contact with a herpes simplex sore. It is passed on through direct contact with an infected person. The virus affects the areas where it enters the body, through activities such as:

- kissing (mouth contact)

- penetrative sex (when the penis enters the vagina, mouth or anus)

- oral sexual contact (from the mouth to the genitals).

Symptoms

These are the same for men and women:

- an itching in the genital or anal area caused by small fluid filled blisters, which burst and leave small sores, which can be very painful; in time they do dry out and scab over. With the first infection they can take two to four weeks to heal properly

- pain when passing urine

- flu-like illness, headache, swollen glands or fever.

Treatment

There is no treatment that can cure herpes, but antiviral medications can shorten and prevent outbreaks during the period of time the person takes the medication.

In addition, daily suppressive therapy for symptomatic herpes can reduce transmission to partners.

Human Immunodeficiency Virus (HIV)

What is it? This is a virus that can damage the body's defence system so that it cannot fight off some infections. If an individual with the HIV virus goes on to get certain serious illnesses, this condition is called AIDS which stands for Acquired Immune Deficiency Syndrome.

How is it spread? HIV is a virus, which can be passed from one person to another in a number of ways, including through sexual contact. Anyone who is sexually active can become infected and as they do, the virus begins to attack their immune system, which is the body's defence against infection. The only way that HIV is passed from one person to another is if the blood, semen, vaginal fluids or breast milk of an infected person enter the body of an uninfected person as follows:

- by having unprotected vaginal, anal or oral sex

- by using a needle or syringe ('works') which has already been used by someone who is infected with HIV

- when a woman with HIV passes the virus to her baby before or during birth, or by breastfeeding.

Symptoms   The symptoms of HIV and AIDS vary, depending on the phase of infection. When first infected with HIV, there may be no symptoms at all, although it's more common to develop a brief flu-like illness two to six weeks after becoming infected.

Because the signs and symptoms of an initial infection, which may include fever, headache, sore throat, swollen lymph glands and rash, are similar to those of other diseases, the HIV infection may not be obvious.

Treatment   At this time, there is no cure for AIDS, but medications are effective in fighting HIV and its complications. Treatments are designed to reduce HIV in the body, keeping the immune system as healthy as possible and decreasing any complications that may develop.

Conclusion

Just skimming the surface of the more common sexually transmitted infections makes clear the further consequences that may be apparent for victims of rape and/or sexual violence. For example, having contracted a virus such as genital herpes can mean that the victim lives with the attack for a lifetime; even if and when the emotional scars have lessened, this physical infection can act as a silent reminder not only in future relationships but if and when a female victim chooses to have a family. When a woman who has the genital herpes virus starts to develop with her baby in her womb, the warts can appear as larger and more painful than ever and so the virus can become a constant reminder of the sexual attacker.

8

Forensic Medical Examination (FME)

First, it is important to outline the procedures that police forces across the country have in place when dealing with both victim and suspect when a serious sexual assault allegation has been raised. There are two main areas: the police role and the examination.

Serious sexual offences to which this procedure relates are defined as:

- rape

- assaults by penetration

- sexual assault involving the use of violence

- any other sexual assault deemed to be serious by the investigating officer

- any attempt to commit any offence listed above.

The police role

Initial response

The police must consider the following five principles during the initial response:

- preservation of life

- preservation of scene(s)

- securing evidence (in particular forensic evidence)

- identification of victim(s) and witness(es)

- identification of suspect(s).

Those responding to any allegation of a serious sexual offence should consider whether the allegation is a critical incident. Even if the allegation amounts to an historic complaint, an immediate response is necessary. If the offence is recent, early and immediate action could preserve vital evidence and possibly prevent further attacks.

Immediate victim care

This initial meeting and how it is handled can determine, to a large extent, not only the ability of the victim to recover from the ordeal, but the subsequent processes of identification, collection and presentation of evidence and their confidence to continue to any criminal proceedings.

From the moment a sexual assault is reported it is important that the victim is treated with tact, sympathy and understanding. Initial questioning will need to obtain information about what has taken place. However, it should be restricted to getting the details of the following:

- the offender (if known)

- the offence

- place of the offence.

The police will then determine if they believe a crime has taken place. It is important that a medical examination takes place as soon as possible, before any detailed questioning. It is important to try to prevent the victim from having a drink or using the toilet until the medical examination has taken place.

Scene preservation and examination

The same principles of scene preservation need to be applied to the scene of a serious sexual offence as those identified in the murder investigation manual. The three principles are as follows:

- identify

- secure

- protect.

All scenes should be identified, secured and protected subject to a full and detailed forensic examination by a trained Forensic Investigator. In each case a senior Forensic Investigator should be consulted to establish a Forensic Strategy for the scene examination and identify the level of resources required. It may also be important to recognise that the scenes of sexual assault may not always be obvious, and particular care should be made to identify all potential scenes. For instance, where the victim was first approached may not be the location of the actual attack. Routes taken by and vehicles travelled in by the suspect or the victim may also be scenes and should be considered for examination. In some cases there may be a number of scenes for consideration. Therefore a clear forensic strategy is vital. Remember also that the victim is classed as a crime scene and may yield forensic evidence. However, in preserving such evidence it is vital to maintain the dignity and confidence of the victim.

The suspect – identification and early arrest

The identification and early arrest of the suspect must always remain a high priority. Where this can be achieved, officers who have not attended the scene or been in contact with the victim should be tasked to affect the arrest. This is to avoid cross contamination. However, it may not always be possible such as in cases where the offender is still at the scene.

Contamination

In such circumstances the level of potential contamination should be recorded and declared to the investigating officer. This will allow the Investigating Officer and Senior Forensic Investigator to be clear about the Forensic Strategy and to enable the discharge of responsibilities under disclosure law. The nature of any cross contamination should be disclosed when submitting samples for forensic analysis.

Suspect is crime scene

The suspect is also a crime scene. Clothing worn or suspected to have been worn by the suspect at the time of the offences should be seized, and where appropriate medical examination and forensic samples from the suspect are to be obtained.

The suspect should not be allowed to wash and must be closely supervised until a decision has been made regarding the recovery of relevant clothing or forensic samples.

Collection of evidence

All possible measures should be taken to prevent cross contamination between victim, suspect and crime scene(s) and in particular, victims and suspect should be:

- attended to by different officers

- transported by different vehicles

- examined at different locations.

Scenes, victims and suspects should beexamined by different scenes of crime officers (SCOs) and forensic medical examiners. Rooms and vehicles used to transport victims and suspects should be cleaned following their use.

The K106 Early Evidence Kit

This does not replace the K105 Full Medical Examination Kit but means that police and allocated organisations can collect samples without physical contact, or having to wait for a medical examiner.

This kit is user friendly and allows urine samples, which can contain vital traces of drugs that would be lost within hours of an alleged attack. Collecting them early will give Forensic Science Services (FSS) toxicology a better chance of finding potential vital evidence.

The mouth swab can be analysed for the detection of semen, which can remain in the mouth for up to two days.

Mouth Kit

The Mouth Kit is used to collect and store forensic samples from the mouth of a complainant suitable for subsequent forensic analysis to detect semen and/or DNA. It contains swabs and containers.

The FSS and Metropolitan Police Service (MPS) developed the K106 in partnership with the aim of increasing the chances of detecting drugs that may have been used to facilitate sexual assault.

Please note: this kit does not replace the taking of urine and mouth samples at the medical examination.

Full forensic medical examination kit

This is a complete forensic kit, which makes possible the efficient salvage of forensic evidence during the forensic medical examination of victims and suspects in sexual offence cases. It is suitable for many types of evidence including alcohol, drugs and DNA. It can also be used for physical evidence such as fibres, hairs or particulates.

Table 8.1 shows the contents of the kit (all in one handy box).

Table 8.1 Full forensic medical examination kit contents

Alcohol/drug blood kit	For collecting and storing a blood sample for subsequent toxicological analysis to detect alcohol, drugs of abuse, medicinal and sedative drugs, including drugs that may be used in a drug facilitated sexual assault. The sample container is manufactured with sufficient preservative and anti-coagulant to ensure the blood is sufficiently preserved until it reaches the forensic laboratory.
Alcohol/drug urine kit	To collect and store a urine sample suitable for subsequent toxicological analysis to detect alcohol, drugs of abuse, medicinal and sedative drugs, including drugs that may be used in a drug facilitated sexual assault. The sample container is manufactured with sufficient preservative to ensure the urine sample is preserved until it reaches the forensic laboratory.
Mouth collection kit	To collect and store forensic samples from the mouth of a complainant suitable for subsequent forensic analysis to detect semen and/or DNA. Contains swabs and containers.

Standard swab kit	Designed for the recovery of body fluids or lubricant from the complainant of sexual assault. The components are suitable for samples requiring analysis using the latest DNA profiling techniques.
Hair collection kit	Allows the recovery of trace evidence such as body fluids, foreign particles or debris from head hair during a forensic medical examination. The product includes a fine toothcomb, scissors, forceps and drapes.
Nail collection kit	To collect and store samples from the fingernails of a complainant or suspect for subsequent forensic analysis of trace evidence such as DNA, fibres, other debris. Contains nail clippers to collect clippings and fine tip swabs to provide greater control to the forensic medical examiner when sampling.
Patient clothing kit	Includes a ground sheet for the patient to stand on whilst undressing and a lightweight gown for the patient to wear once undressed. The gown material is opaque with a large overlap to provide discretion for the patient and short sleeves make it easier for the patient to be examined. The material has been selected to minimise fibre shedding.
Couch cover kit	Provides a barrier between the patient and the couch where an intimate examination is carried out as part of a forensic medical examination. Contains a single couch cover, which is free from all types of trace evidence. The sheet is designed to fit on a medical couch and comes with elasticised corners to prevent slippage.
Medical examination forms kit	Contains the necessary paperwork for use during the forensic medical examination of a complainant or suspect where forensic samples are collected. Each pack contains four separate sheets.
Body outline forms kit	Body outline diagrams, for the examiner to record observations with regard to injuries or bruising noted during a forensic medical examination of a complainant or suspect. Contains 14 different diagrams.
Emergency information kit	Victim information pack, which includes: ACPO Booklet: 'Help for those who have been Sexually Assaulted', AFP 'What happens now?' booklet, BPAS 'Emergency contraceptive pills leaflet'.
Sterile water kit	For use as a wetting agent on dried forensic samples. Includes four ampoules of 10ml sterile water, featuring easy to open twist caps.

Other forensic testing equipment, which can be used in conjunction with any of the above, is shown in Table 8.2.

Table 8.2 Additional forensic testing equipment

Car seat cover kit	To provide a barrier between the passenger and the car seat when transporting complainants or suspects. Prevents transfer of evidence types, such as fibres, hairs, particulates and DNA. Elasticised corners make it easier to fit any car seat.
Condom collection kit	To collect and store physical evidence types found on condoms, femidons and sanitary wear (this could include concealed packages). These items may be removed during a forensic medical examination or taken from the scene of crime. Contains a pair of disposable forceps to prevent handling of the item, which preserves any fingerprints, which may be present. Also a clip to prevent leakage of any potential evidence.
Proctoscope kit (available in three sizes)	To enable an anal examination and the accurate recovery of appropriate swabs for subsequent forensic analysis. The medical grade plastic ensures exceptional strength and provides safety and reliability for the patient and user. The smooth edges ensure comfort for the patient.
Sterile water	For use as a wetting agent on dried forensic samples. Includes four ampoules of 10ml sterile water, featuring easy to open twist caps.
Sanitary wear collection kit	To collect and store items of sanitary wear worn by a complainant during or after a sexual assault for subsequent forensic analysis to detect body fluids, DNA, lubricants or other contact traces. May also be used for the storage of toilet paper if offered by the patient as a sample, or to submit concealed packages for forensic examination.
Speculum kit (available in three sizes)	Used to retain the vagina in an open position for procedures of the vaginal/cervical area.
Anal – vaginal – penile swab kits	To collect and store forensic vaginal samples for subsequent forensic analysis to detect body fluids and/or DNA, lubricants or other contact traces.

During the FME with the alleged victim or the alleged suspect, the examination is conducted with a forensic medical examiner accompanied by a specially trained police officer. The same forensic medical examination kit should *not* be used for both to prevent contamination.

The medical needs of the victim will be treated as a high priority. Reasonable steps to minimise the movement of the victim and therefore minimise the trauma should therefore be taken. The whole process will be expedited as quickly as possible to take into consideration the distress caused to the victim.

Protective clothing will be worn by the FME and SCO and anyone else who is present at the FME to ensure that there is no cross-contamination of evidence from their clothing.

Evidence

It is the responsibility of the trained police officer to ensure appropriate packaging, labelling and continuity of samples. They will ensure that items are deposited into the appropriate secure storage and that the appropriate forms are completed at the time of examination, with full details of each sample or exhibit.

9

Rape and the Law

All serious sexual offence cases have to be tried in the Crown Court. Judges presiding over these cases have to be 'ticketed', which means they have to undergo certain training authorising them to judge specific cases.

There are effectively four levels of Crown Court Judge and four classifications of offence according to their seriousness. First there are the High Court Judges, who can deal with any case within the jurisdiction of the Crown Court, but who, in theory, try the most serious and difficult cases, for example: treason and murder (Class 1) and manslaughter and rape (Class 2). Second are the 'ticketed' Circuit Judges. These are judges of experience who are variously authorised to try certain (Class 1 and 2) cases, mainly murder and rape, and also by reason of its special difficulty and complexity, serious fraud (mainly Class 3). Many Circuit Judges now have an authorisation of one or more sorts, and authorised 'murder' and 'rape' judges now try the bulk of murders and rapes and other serious sexual offences. Third there are the Circuit Judges who, whether 'ticketed' or not, try the main range of work as in (Classes 3 and 4), some of which, for example, are drug trafficking, armed robberies and frauds of various sorts, of great seriousness and difficulty. Fourth there are Recorders who, depending on their experience and ability, may try work of various levels of seriousness, including rape (Class 2) and offences as in (Class 3 and 4), but usually the less serious and, because they only sit for a week or so at a time, the shorter cases. The Senior Presiding Judge, on behalf of the Lord Chief Justice, authorises selected recorders to hear cases involving rape or a serious sexual offence. Before being authorised, a judge must have wide and significant experience of the criminal justice system and must have demonstrated the necessary sensitivity for these cases. These authorised Recorders may not hear such a case without first having attended the appropriate Judicial Studies Board Training, and the designated course for this is the Serious Sexual Offences Seminar (SSO). Authorised Recorders along with other authorised Judiciary will be invited to continuation training every three years from the date of their first attendance.

England and Wales is almost unique in its extensive reliance on part-time judges, Recorders, in the exercise of criminal and civil jurisdiction in its higher courts. Practitioners are eligible for appointment as a Recorder if they have had a right of audience in the Crown or County Courts for ten years or more.

Consent is an important factor in any rape case; consent is often absent due to duress arising from the use of violence, overwhelming intimidation or aggression or because the victim is under the influence of drugs or alcohol, or it may be that the victim was underage or did not have mental capacity to fend off the perpetrator.

Rape and consent

The Sexual Offences Act outlines that Assault by penetration is has been redefined to include that it is an offence for a male or female to penetrate the vagina or anus of another person without their consent. Penetration can be by a part of the body, e.g. fingers, or anything else that is not a body part, used for the purpose of penetration (with sexual intent).

There are three new measures on the issue of consent:

- There is a statutory definition on the issue of consent: a person consents if he or she agrees by choice to the sexual activity and has the freedom and capacity to make that choice.

- All the circumstances at the time of the offence will be looked at in determining whether the defendant is reasonable in believing the complainant consented.

- People will be considered most unlikely to have agreed to sexual activity if they were subject to threats or fear of serious harm, unconscious, drugged, abducted, or unable to communicate because of a physical disability.

Measures are designed to redress the balance in favour of victims without prejudicing the defendant's right to a fair trial, to help juries reach just and fair decisions on what is a difficult area or prosecution.

New consent law

Guidance that came into force in January 2015 means that perpetrators of rape must be able to prove that their target gave consent. This is more robust than 'no means no', because it covers unconsciousness, being drugged or under the influence of alcohol to name but a few shady areas.[1]

Victims' Right to Review Scheme

The Victims' Right to Review was launched by the Crown Prosecution Service (CPS) in June 2013. This scheme is intended to make it easier for victims to seek answers about their case and why it may have been terminated or withheld.[2]

Many thousands of people affected by rape and sexual violence have had their cases dropped, listed as a no crime or terminated without really being given the full reason. If nothing else, this is an avenue for victims to be more informed about decisions being made about them, their life and the rationale behind it.

---

1   For more information follow this link: www.cps.gov.uk/news/latest_news/cps_and_police_focus_on_consent_at_first_joint_national_rape_conference/

2   Information about this scheme and the revised Victim's Code which came into effect in December 2010, can be found at www.cps.gov.uk/victims_witnesses/victims_right_to_review/

For the purposes of trial in the Crown Court offences are classified as follows.

Class 1

(a) Misprision of treason and treason felony;

(b) Murder;

(c) Genocide;

(d) Torture, hostage-taking and offences under the War Crimes Act 1991;

(e) An offence under the Official Secrets Acts;

(f) Manslaughter;

(g) Infanticide;

(h) Child destruction;

(i) Abortion (section 58 of the Offences against the Person Act 1861);

(j) Sedition;

(k) An offence under section 1 of the Geneva Conventions Act 1957;

(l) Mutiny;

(m) Piracy;

(n) Soliciting, incitement, attempt or conspiracy to commit any of the above offences.

Class 2

(a) Rape;

(b) Sexual intercourse with a girl under 13;

(c) Incest with girl under 13;

(d) Assault by penetration;

(e) Causing a person to engage in sexual activity, where penetration is involved;

(f) Rape of a child under 13;

(g) Assault of a child under 13 by penetration;

(h) Causing or inciting a child under 13 to engage in sexual activity, where penetration is involved;

(i) Sexual activity with a person with a mental disorder, where penetration is involved;

(j) Inducement to procure sexual activity with a mentally disordered person where penetration is involved;

(k) Paying for sexual services of a child where child is under 13 and penetration is involved;

(l) Committing an offence with intent to commit a sexual offence, where the offence is kidnapping or false imprisonment;

(m) Soliciting, incitement, attempt or conspiracy to commit any of the above offences.

Class 3

All other offences not listed in classes 1 or 2.

Special measures

It's not that long ago that the only special measures in place in the courtroom for a victim of rape and/or sexual violence were a chair and a box of tissues. Nowadays, these issues are taken much more seriously and more is offered in the form of some of the following special measures:

- screens – to ensure that the witness does not see the defendant

- live link – allowing a witness to give evidence from outside the courtroom

- evidence in private – clearing the court of most people (legal representatives and certain others must be allowed to stay)

- removal of wigs and gowns – by judges, advocates and so on (only applicable in the Crown Court)

- video-recorded evidence in chief – allowing an interview with the witness, which has been video-recorded before the trial, to be shown as the witness's evidence in chief

- intermediaries – allowing an approved intermediary to help a witness communicate with the police, legal representatives and the court.

In law the rape victim has no status as a 'victim'. If he/she is required to give evidence, he/she has the status of witness. Once an offence has been reported, it is up to the police to investigate and the CPS to determine whether the case can proceed to the Court.

The police role

The police will usually work with the following procedure throughout the court procedure:

- Inform complainants if there is not going to be an investigation into the crime *within five* days of the crime being reported.

- Provide a copy of, or make sure of access to the local 'victims of crime' leaflet.

- Refer victim details to a voluntary organisation such as Victim Support, unless the victim asks them not to do so.

- Keep complainant/victim updated on a monthly basis, until the case is closed.

- Tell the complainant/victim if there is a possibility that the case may be reviewed at a later date and ask if information on any review is required.

- Provide information if someone is arrested within one day if victims are receiving the enhanced service or within five days for other victims.

- Provide information when they release a suspect on bail including if there are any bail conditions and when those conditions are altered within one day if the complainant/victim is receiving the enhanced service, or within five days for other victims.

- Provide information regarding any decision they take to charge or not to charge a suspect within one day if receiving the enhanced service or within five days for other victims.

Her Majesty's Courts Service Staff will do the following:

- provide information about court dates and case outcomes to the Witness Care Unit and the police, so that they can keep the complainant/victim updated

- ensure that the victim/complainant and defendant have a separate waiting areas and seat in the courtroom away from the defendant's family, where possible

- make every attempt to ensure that the victim/complainant does not have to wait more than two hours to give evidence

- provide an information point at the court where possible so that the victim/complainant can find out what is happening in the case.[3]

Witness Care Unit

The CPS determines whether the case investigated and prepared by the police can proceed to Court. The first test applied by the CPS is whether there is sufficient evidence for a realistic prospect of conviction, and the second is whether it is in the public interest for the case to go to Court. The victim interest is a part of the public interest criteria. Some of the public interest factors that can affect the victims, which are likely to bend towards a prosecution, are:

- where a conviction is likely to result in a significant sentence

- where a weapon was used or violence was threatened

---

3   The Code of Practice for Victims of Crime: A Guide for Victims can be obtained at www.homeoffice.gov.uk

- where the victim of the offence was vulnerable, had been put in considerable fear or suffered personal attack

- where there are grounds for believing that the offence is likely to be continued or repeated.

The victim of crime is regarded as an ordinary member of the public with a responsibility to assist the police with the provision of evidence, and when that evidence is needed as part of the prosecution process, to act as a witness in court.

As witnesses for the prosecution, victims are not provided with their own legal representation in court and may not have been introduced to the prosecution barrister prior to giving their evidence.

The Witness Care Unit/Service provides support from a trained volunteer from the Witness Service before going to court, and a volunteer will be at the court to assist a witness. They cannot discuss evidence or give legal advice, but they will be a friendly face who will show the witness around the court and provide information about what will happen.

There is a Witness Service in every criminal court in England and Wales. This service is run by the independent national charity Victim Support and it helps victims and witnesses (both prosecution and defence) and their families and friends, before, during and after the trial. The Witness Service sends a leaflet to witnesses before the court hearing to offer its services.

The CPS

The Sexual Offences Act is split into two parts, the first devoted to sexual offences, creating new offences and widening the scope of existing ones, and the second covering offenders with an emphasis on the protection of vulnerable individuals.

It provides clear and coherent differences in sex offences to protect individuals from abuse and exploitation, and is designed to be fair and non-discriminatory.

Government updates

Reproduced under Crown Copyright requirements:

**Convicting rapists and protecting victims –
Government announces new measures**

28 Nov 2007

The Solicitor General, Vera Baird today announced the response to the Government's consultation paper on convicting rapists and protecting victims – the results of which will play an important part in improving the outcome for victims in rape cases.

A number of significant measures will have an impact on how rape cases are heard in court, these include:

- Allowing adult victims of rape to give video-recorded evidence at trials.

- To consider further how general expert material could be presented in a controlled and consistent way with a view to dispelling myths around rape victims' behaviour.

- Defining the law on a complainant's capacity to give consent where drink or drugs are involved – to assist judges and juries.

- Ensuring that all relevant evidence of complaints made by victims in rape cases should be admissible as evidence in a trial, irrespective of time passed since the alleged conduct Criminal justice and courts bill 2014–- points of interest.

- Ending of automatic early release for paedophiles and terrorists.

- Banning violent rape pornography.

Home Office Minister Vernon Coaker said:

The measures announced today are the latest in a series of steps the Government has taken towards tackling this deplorable crime. By investing more money than ever before in victim support, rolling out nationwide specialist officers and rape prosecutors and allowing the courts to set tougher sentences the message is clear: we are committed to ensuring that victims are supported and that offenders are subject to the full force of the law.

The consultation has been an extremely valuable process and we have looked carefully at each contribution. Everyone who submitted their views deserves our thanks.

Justice Minister Maria Eagle said:

To secure confidence, the CJS must earn confidence of the rape victim as well as the victim of the burglary or the mugging. To narrow the 'justice gap' we must tackle the gap between the number of rapes and the number of convictions.

All the parts of the system need to work together to ensure rape victims get the support they need and get justice to ensure that perpetrators know they can't get away with it.

The new CJS Strategic Plan makes clear that improving the criminal justice response to serious sexual offences should be a priority and that local criminal justice boards should work together - strengthening partnerships between chief constables and chief crown prosecutors and courts, prison and probation.

Attorney General, Baroness Scotland said:

As well as being one of the most devastating crimes that continues to affect our communities, rape remains one of the most difficult crimes when it comes to the courtroom.

I am personally committed to the measures announced today. We have to tackle rape and those who commit this horrific crime with a strengthening in the law. Equally we have to ensure that victims of this horrific crime have enough confidence in the Criminal Justice System to not only come forward, but to be willing to take the case to court.

Michelle Bernasconi from the Victims Advisory Panel (VAP) said:

The VAP welcomes the government's response to improving the trial process for rape victims. We (the VAP) have been working with a number of CJS agencies and voluntary organisations to improve understanding of the impact of rape on individual victims.

What impact will the reforms have?

- *Video evidence:* Enabling the jury to see and hear a rape victim being interviewed at the time of complaint by means of a video-recorded statement used as evidence-in-chief, will usually provide more compelling and coherent evidence than that given in court several months later. This would of course be subject to the victim agreeing to give evidence in this manner.

- *Expert evidence:* We know from the Amnesty 2005 Poll that myths around rape are prevalent and entrenched. It is desirable for juries to have information concerning the psychological reactions of rape victims. We will look for a fair way to present such information to juries other than through evidence presented by the prosecution or defence. The judgment in the case of Bree made this clear. It stated that a person may lack the capacity to consent when they are intoxicated, even if they are still conscious.

- *Hearsay; first complaint evidence:* The Government will legislate to make victims' complaints to other people that they have been raped, admissible as evidence in criminal trials in *all circumstances.* (At present, evidence of what somebody told somebody else is not normally admissible as evidence.)

The Government's Rape Consultation is just part of the wider strategy to put rape victims' needs first and bring rapists to justice:

- We have introduced Specialist Officers and specialist Rape Prosecutors across England and Wales and are introducing specialist training for police, prosecutors and barristers acting in rape cases.

- We have put in place new arrangements for the performance management of police forces and the CPS on rape. The new Criminal Justice Public Service Agreement and indicators for CJ agencies will make clear that rape should be a national and local priority.

- All forces are receiving operational support to develop and deliver action plans to improve rape investigation strategies and implement recommendations from *Without Consent [2007 rape inspection].*

- Withdrawal is a major cause of attrition in rape cases so we need to ensure victims are supported through the criminal justice process. This year we are spending around £3m (bringing total to £10m over four years and up from around £400k in 2001—02) to supplement local funding, on:

- Extending the network of Sexual Assault Referral Centre's (where victims receive medical care and counselling and can assist the police investigation through a forensic examination). Since 2010 there are now 30 – 40 SARCS throughout England and Wales offering different levels of support to those affected by rape and sexual violence. Some of these only support those who are intending to prosecute while the larger SARCs offer much more for those in need whether they are a witness in a criminal investigation or needing somewhere to talk and be heard.

- Piloting Independent Sexual Violence Advisors in 38 areas to provide advocacy and support for victims.

- Providing funding through the Victims Fund for voluntary organisations supporting victims of sexual violence.

• The Sexual Offences Act 2003 provides a coherent and comprehensive set of offences appropriate for the modern day, and strengthened the law by creating a definition of consent and removing the defence that a person could avoid conviction for rape if he had an honest but mistaken belief in consent.

• The Domestic Violence, Crime and Victims Act 2004 provides for a statutory victims Code of Practice, placing obligations on the police to keep victims informed of case progress; The Youth Justice and Criminal Evidence Act 1999 introduced specific provisions for vulnerable and intimidated witnesses, including video links and screens.

10

Sex Offender Patterns of Behaviour and the Sex Offenders Register

The maximum sentence for rape is life imprisonment. However, the number of rapes across the country appears to be ever increasing and sexual predators seem to be at every corner. The newspapers bring new stories of rape and sexual violence on a daily basis. Monthly showings of *Crimewatch* expose case after case of this brutal crime.

Preconditions

There are five preconditions for rape and/or sexual violence that the sex offender needs to have in place:

- The individual does not adhere to any code of right or wrong.

- The individual wants to sexually abuse (has a fantasy e.g. sex attack)

- The individual is able to find ways of overcoming core boundaries (making it right in their own head).

- The individual finds ways of overcoming environmental boundaries (distorted thinking patterns).

- The individual is able to find a way of overcoming the victim's resistance (charm – power and/or control, e.g. using weapons or other threatening behaviour).

The offender fantasises about their particular victim, for example a nurse. This is clearly represented by the following example:

1. **The individual wants to sexually abuse (has a fantasy sex attack).**

   In this case the perpetrator would seek out a place where nurses are frequently found.

2. **The individual is able to find ways of overcoming core boundaries (making it right in their head).**

   The perpetrator sees the 'target' and the fantasy rehearsal increases.

3. **The individual who finds ways of overcoming environmental boundaries (distorted thinking patterns).**

   The perpetrator seeks ways of making his/her fantasy become a reality by finding a place to hide, getting past any security measures in place and totally ignoring any concept of whether the target is in agreement. His need is to feel powerful and controlling.

4. **The individual is able to find a way of overcoming the target's resistance (charm – power and/or control, e.g. using weapons or other threatening behaviour).**

   He/she takes their chance and the attack is imminent.

As in chapter four, we again work from and demonstrate the basics of the Finkelhor Precondition Model. The elements to offend give an example of what is considered as 'stranger rape'. The preconditions are very similar in cases of drug facilitated sexual assault, acquaintance rape and sexual violation within families and relationships. The only part that would change is the target (see Figure 10.1).

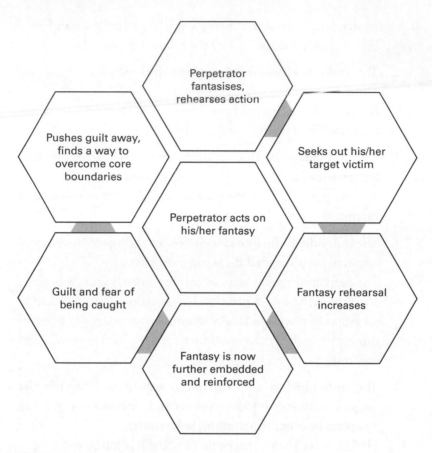

Figure 10.1 The pattern of rape

This shows a classic cycle of sex offender behaviour and distorted thinking patterns. The behaviour is constantly fed by each fantasy and by each rehearsal of that fantasy and further embedded and reinforced by one or more offence, as and when they are committed.

Sexually abusive behaviours

These can be defined as follows:

- Incest: inappropriate sexual behaviour within families

- Exhibitionism: indecent exposure, flashing, masturbation

- Molestation: touching and fondling

- Rape: intercourse without consent

- Voyeurism: secretly spying on/photographing others for sexual gratification

- Frottage: Rubbing up against others for sexual gratification

- Verbal sexual intimidation: constantly referring to sexuality during conversation.

Female perpetrators

Female perpetrators are out there and we have noticed an increasing number of clients in recent years who have related their experiences as children.

Female perpetrators generally fall into the following categories:

- Facilitators: women who intentionally aid men in gaining access to children for sexual purposes

- Reluctant partners: women in long-term relationships who go along with sexual exploitation of a minor out of fear of being abandoned

- Initiating partner: women who want to sexually offend against a child, and who may do it themselves or get a man or another woman to do it while they watch

- Seducers and lovers: women who direct their sexual interest towards adolescents and develop an intense attachment

- Paedophiles: women who desire an exclusive and sustained sexual relationship with a child (a very rare occurrence)

- Psychotic: women who suffer from a mental illness and who have inappropriate sexual contact with children as a result.

Women who might feel inadequate or unable to maintain an adult relationship with either gender may put their children in the role of substitute lover. Female perpetrators can come from any background. Patterns of behaviour such as this can elicit a cycle of generational abuse, as each family member learns behaviour that is considered 'normal', perpetuating an ever increasing cycle of systematic familial abuse.

For many years there has been an overriding myth about sexual perpetrators and paedophiles, giving the impression that these individuals have a certain look about them, dress in the same way or hide in dark corners lying in wait for their target. This can be a comfort to all of us, giving us a 'safe' feeling of knowing who is dangerous to our children, to our loved ones.

History shows that from the many high profile cases of child abduction and sexual deviation towards children as well as the rapes and murders of innocent women across the globe that they look just like everyone else.

Sex Offenders Register

There are a number of legislations governing the obligations of a registered sex offender. Most notable are the Part 1 of the Sex Offences Act 1997, which came into being on the 1 September 1997 and Part 2 of the Sexual Offences Act 2003, which came into effect on 1 May 2004. The latter cancelled out all previous legislation and re-introduced most 1997 provisions with some improvements. All registered offenders are bound by the conditions of the 2003 Act; irrespective of whether their conviction was prior to the act coming in to force.

The obligations are that they must:

(a) Register at a designated Police Station within three days of conviction or caution.

(b) Offenders will have to notify a change of address or personal details within three days of the change taking place.

(c) Offenders will have to notify of any address they reside for more than seven days or more, whether that is seven consecutive or seven days in a 12-month period.

(d) All offenders will have to re-confirm their notified details annually, (periodic notification).

(e) All notifications will have to be made in person and the police may take fingerprints and photograph at initial notification.

(f) Offenders will have to produce their National Insurance Number at initial notification. Those already on the register will have to notify NI number when they first notify change of details after commencement of the 2003 Act.

Under existing legislation, registered sex offenders are required to notify the police of any travel outside the UK which is for three days or more. This requirement was introduced by the Sexual Offences Act 2003 (Travel Notification Requirements) Regulations 20045 by virtue of powers under section 86 of the SOA 2003.

The offender must notify this information no less than seven days before the date of intended departure (or as soon as reasonably practicable) and not less than 24 hours before that date.

New Crime and Policy Bill 2015

This bill lists changes to the current sex offender existing civil orders. Two current civil orders are being replaced, and they are the sexual offender's prevention order and foreign travel order. The Sexual Harm Prevention Order (SHPO) will replace both. There are further changes such as a Sexual Risk Order (SRO) which replaces the risk of sexual harm order.[1]

Qualifying offences for the Sex Offenders Register

These are as follows:

- Rape (S1 SOA 1956)

- Intercourse with a girl under 13 (S5 SOA 1956)

- Intercourse with a girl under 16 (S5 SOA 1956), if the offender was over 20

---

1 You can download the factsheet at www.gov.uk/government/uploads/system/uploads/attachment_data/file/251341/27__28_sexual_offences_and_VOO_fact_sheet.pdf

- Incest by a man (S10 SOA 1956) if the victim or the other party was under 18

- Buggery (Anal penetration) (S12 SOA 1956), if the offender was over 20 and the victim or other party was under 18

- Indecency between men (S13 SOA 1956) if offender over 20 and victim or other party was under 18

- Indecent assault on a woman (S14 SOA 1956), if the victim was under 18 and/or the offender was sentenced to imprisonment for 30 months or more or admitted to hospital subject to a restriction order

- Indecent assault on a man (S15 SOA 1956), if the victim was under 18 and/or the offender was sentenced to imprisonment for 30 months or more or admitted to hospital subject to a restriction order

- Assault with the intent to commit buggery (S16 SOA 1956), if the victim or other party was under 18

- Causing or encouraging the prostitution of, intercourse with or indecent assault on a girl under 16 (S28 SOA 1956)

- Indecent conduct towards a child (S1 Indecency with Children Act 1960)

- Inciting a girl under 16 to have incestuous sexual intercourse (S54 CLA 1997)

- Indecent photographs or pseudo-photographs if the photographs or pseudo-photographs showed a child under 16 (S1 of the Protection of Children Act 1978) the offender must be over 18 and is sentenced in respect of the offence to imprisonment for a term of at least 12 months

There are many more as outlined in SOA 2003, Part 2.

Regulations and notifications for travel outside the UK

A registered sex offender has a number of obligations to fulfil before he/she leaves the country. He/she needs to give the following information:

- the date of departure from the UK

- the destination country (or, if there is more than one, the first)

- the point of arrival in that country

- his/her point/s of arrival in any countries he/she will be visiting in addition to the initial destination

- the carrier/s he/she intends to use to leave the UK or any other points of arrival, while he/she is outside the UK but not internal flights

- details of his/her accommodation arrangements for his/her first night outside the UK

- his/her date of re-entry to the UK

- his/her point of arrival on his/her return to the UK.

The rules have tightened up somewhat and can be found detailed in the following document: www.gov.uk/government/news/tightening-the-law-on-sex-offenders

In August 2012, it was a Statutory Instrument Paper; 2012 No. 1876 – Criminal Law, England and Wales. The Sexual Offences Act 2003 (Notifications Requirements) (England and Wales) Regulations 2012, which implemented changes to the notification requirements.

When a person convicted of a sexual offence is listed on the Sex Offenders Register, they have to complete a Sex Offenders Notification Form, Part 2 of the Sexual Offences Act 2003. This form and all parts of the Act are subject to change and updates can be obtained accordingly, via the government website.

This form needs to be completed with a police officer or other authorised person at a prescribed police station upon conviction. In a nutshell, the form includes such details as:

- specification of type or reason for notification

- (conviction) notification details

- contact details

- National Insurance details
- notification of any residence with a child for at least 12 hours or more in one period
- photographs and fingerprints
- passport details
- vehicle/s details
- changes to any details of the above.

The offender is informed that his/her movements may be monitored. Signatures of both the completing police officer/authorised person and the offender are required. All bank and credit/debit card and any building society or post office details are taken. The Failure to Comply notice also needs to be read thoroughly and signed by the offender.

Those whose job it is to manage sex offenders may also use additional SOA Notification Requirements Forms to ensure that the sex offender understands exactly what is expected of them. Please see a sample of such in Appendices 11 and 12 – for information purposes only.

Sex offenders who are convicted and sent to prison are able to engage in a variety of offender behaviour programmes (OBPs). These programmes are developed and in place to reduce reoffending. Programmes specifically aimed at sex offenders are called sex offender treatment programmes (SOTP) which offer varying levels according to the risk and need of the sex offender. There are many of these programmes available up and down the UK. The programmes cover cognitive, motivational behaviour change, patterns of thinking, skill development and goal setting.[2]

---

2   Further information about such programmes can be found at www.justice.gov. uk/offenders/before-after-release

Paedophile vigilante groups

In the last five to six years, paedophile vigilante groups have excelled in their internet operation as they continually track paedophile activity across the UK. Vigilante groups set up as children and teenagers on various social media websites. They converse using teenage vocabulary with potential paedophiles and sex offenders who are grooming and arranging to meet their target disguised as children and/or teenagers themselves.

Different police forces appear to have published mixed views on the vigilante groups. However, it cannot be denied that their efforts in creating CD evidence of each set of messages and following and confronting the paedophiles when arranging to meet children and teenagers have greatly increased the conviction rate of this crime.

As adults it can be difficult enough to keep a watchful eye on fake social media profiles, scam emails and personal cloning, but for children and young people the dangers are one hundredfold.

The very fact that these groups are in operation at all is testament to the continuous, manipulative preying upon children of both sexes. There are mixed feelings about the vigilante groups, some negative and some positive. However, my view is that anything that prevents child abuse and adults preying on children can only be regarded as progress.

11

Reflective Case Histories

Marcia

Marcia was in a relationship with Eddie for 18 months, and they had a good time to begin with. After three months he said he wanted to take her on holiday abroad, as she'd often said that she'd never been on an aeroplane.

She was in awe of everything from the plane to actually staying in a hotel. After only 48 hours, as they were walking along a deserted beach just having enjoyed a wonderful evening out, Eddie got rough with Marcia and threw her to the ground. When she said she didn't want sex, right there and then he raped her in the sand, got up and walked off, leaving her to find her own way back to their hotel.

When she finally found her way back to the hotel, Eddie was asleep. Heart sinking and being such a long way from home, she considered what she could do now. He had all the money and the tickets to get home. So, after a long hot shower, feeling scared, lost and alone, she slept out on the sofa so as not to wake him. As the morning came, he quietly made coffee and sat down on the edge of the sofa, staring at her.

Head in hands, he was saying he was sorry and that he didn't know what had come over him; he had felt rejected, and his love for her was so strong that he just lost control. As tears soaked through his fingers, Marcia felt deeply saddened and pulled him close to her.

Weeks turned into months, and mostly he was kind and considerate, but every now and again after an alcohol-fuelled night out with his mates or a day at a football match, Eddie would change into a sexual monster, holding her down to force sex upon her, and if she dared to say no or fight him off it would just get worse for her, culminating in being beaten as well as raped.

She quickly learned that it was easier for her to keep quiet, knowing that it would soon be over and he would fall asleep. It never finished soon enough for her, and she became emotionally numbed by the way he treated her.

One night after a long day at a football match, Eddie attacked Marcia, grabbing her hair he woke her from sleep, and as she lay beneath him he held her tiny neck in his hand. She started to feel faint and knew that if he really wanted to he could just snap her neck and kill her right there and then. Luckily for her he didn't, and judging by the way he collapsed next to her he'd obviously had too much to drink. As he began to fall into a deep sleep, Marcia crept out of the room and taking her earlier packed case walked out of his life forever.

Over the previous six weeks she had been talking to a local women's organisation and after much support from them and those she'd met there, they taught her about having an escape plan. From somewhere within her she found the courage to leave Eddie and started a new life in a new county many miles from him.

It always seems so unfair that a person, male or female, should have to move away from everything they know and love, all that is familiar, to escape the controlling violent or sexual behaviours of another, but sometimes for them it's the only way to be free.

Melanie

The gang that raped her daughter can only be described as cool, calculating and extremely predatory, says Angela, Melanie's mother. Melanie, a softly spoken dental nurse, was invited to

Newcastle for a two-day training event by some of her college friends. She tells us:

> On the Thursday night we went to a wine bar near the hotel, I was determined not to drink too much as I needed a clear head for the next day's training. We were sat at a table in view of a glass door, and I noticed a group of lads walking by. They were looking at my friends and me and came into the bar. They all smiled and went off to another part of the wine bar, and I took no further notice. Looking back I now realise that what happened later was a brutal and calculated attack and the group of lads were in fact sexual predators, preying on lone girls and women.
>
> We were dancing, enjoying ourselves, one of the group of lads came over and started to dance up close to me, he was trying to talk to me. Then another of the group came up to do the same and the first one went away. I smiled and mouthed 'thank you'. He introduced himself as Charlie. After a few laughs and smiles, he returned to the group of which there were about nine lads. None of the group bothered any of us again, until it was time to leave.

Melanie says she only had three bottles of light lager and felt okay, and then Charlie appeared and invited her to a club that his mate owned.

> My friends were tired and wanted to leave and go back to the hotel. I felt that I had no need not to trust Charlie. He had been the perfect gent, and I was keen to go to the club and have some fun. I promised not to be too long and that I would see them back at the hotel soon.

When she arrived at the club, Charlie's friends were already there and asked what she wanted to drink. She asked for a light lager. After about 20 minutes Melanie started to feel quite odd. She went to the dance floor with Charlie and his friends, and she remembers feeling clumsy.

She says the music seemed to get louder, but she was unable to coordinate with the beat, almost as if her brain was not connected to her body.

The group kept offering Melanie more drinks, but she said no, because she knew she didn't feel right. She had no idea at that point that she had been drugged, and the chemicals were starting to take effect.

> I just felt exhausted every time I sat down and Charlie or one of his friends would heave me back up and try to dance with me.

Melanie knew she needed her phone and remembers being barely able to focus as she saw Charlie holding her phone and waving it at her, smiling. The rest of her memory of that night is disjointed and hazy, and she couldn't quite connect her feet to her head.

At some point she recalls being outside feeling the cold air on her face and then the motion of being in a car. She had no recollection of how or when she got into a car. She remembers that she could feel hands all over her in that car. Melanie has a vague recollection of a hotel room, where there were at least six men waiting who she had not seen before. The rest of the night was a collection of sickening sexual assault and the worst kind of brutality imaginable.

Melanie realised at one point that the men were not speaking English, but she could not make out what language it was. Sometime later Melanie became slightly more coherent and screamed for them to stop and to leave her alone. At this point she remembers one of the Englishmen saying, 'She is boring me now, we have to get her out.'

She was bundled into a car again and recalls the men laughing and jeering at her. They dropped her off at the kerb outside the hotel she was staying in. Somehow she managed to get in and stumble to her room.

Melanie got to her room and slid down the wall and onto the floor. What seemed like hours later (but was in fact, only a matter of minutes) one of her friends was knocking at the door. She said she would call the police, but Melanie didn't want her to. She says she was just too scared.

Sophie her friend, talked her round, convincing her that it was the right thing to do. The police came within half an hour. She consented to an early evidence kit examination, so that any immediate evidence could be kept. Carefully labelling and bagging all of the clothes she was wearing, they took her to a victim suite where a full forensic medical examination was carried out.

The test showed that Melanie had been drugged using Rohypnol. Due to there being more than one assailant, there were obviously several sets of DNA results, and the police managed to locate six of the men in question. The men colluded in saying that Melanie had consented to sex with all of the men.

The case was due to be heard at Crown Court but the CPS later dropped charges just ten days before the trial was set to begin. The reasons for dropping the case were as follows:

1. CCTV from the nightclub had shown Melanie dancing with the group.

2. Melanie went to the club of her own choice.

3. Melanie allowed the men to give her a lift to her hotel.

Melanie was subjected to a secondary injury in that she felt not believed by the CPS. She later resorted to self-harming behaviours in order to self-punish for the fact that she had 'allowed' herself to be assaulted by simply going out for a night, by accepting a lift. Melanie wanted desperately to feel normal, even, she says, if it was a 'new kind of normal' as suggested by the therapist. She invested a lot of her time and energy in the processing of the incident, and she started to see that she wasn't to blame, that the responsibility lay with the attackers. She felt that she needed to move away and start a new life, where she would not be recognised or see anything about the attack. She now lives a long way away and is happily married with three children.

Martin

Martin was good friends with his neighbours, Mary and Sean; they were Irish and hadn't been in the country long. One evening they phoned and invited Martin over on the following Friday for a curry and a few bottles of wine to celebrate their new venture of taking over the local sandwich shop. Martin was delighted to accept and looked forward to the evening. He had been working hard all week and could do with a break and a bit of relaxation. Friday evening came, and he got in from his job as a roofer, got changed and made his way over to Sean and Mary's house.

The meal was great and some other friends of Sean's turned up. Martin had a few glasses of wine and soon began to feel a bit odd, as he wasn't used to drinking so much. Mary got called away to her mother's, so it just left the lads, and the night turned into a bit of a party. One of Sean's friends, 'Mick', was a bit pushy and kept asking him if he'd ever had sex with a bloke before. Martin got quite offended but couldn't find it in himself to argue or say what he thought.

Mick went and got Martin a glass of 'water' and said he ought to go and lay down upstairs for a bit until the giddiness disappeared. Martin did just that and was sick in the toilet on the way up the stairs. When he made it into the spare bedroom, Mick was already waiting there with another of his friends, Jason. Martin went to run out, but they both grabbed him and ripped at his trousers. Martin was stunned and very drunk, but he fought them off as much as he could.

Both men raped Martin that night, and as he fell into his house later, he was shaking uncontrollably. He had no idea that could happen to a bloke, let alone a bloke of his size, his build. He felt so stupid. Was he gay? Had all those conquests down at the local club with all those gorgeous women meant nothing to his masculinity?

Martin decided to say nothing to anyone and let it go. He stopped seeing Mary and Sean and couldn't face going out. It got to the point where he was drinking so much on his own at home at night that he started to get to work late and often didn't turn up at all. He lost interest in life until one Saturday afternoon he had no choice but to go to the chemist to get some painkillers for one of his many hungover and wrung-out mornings. While he was there, he saw something that he couldn't take his eyes off; it was a poster that read 'Have you been a victim of sexual assault?' Martin blinked back to normal for a minute, quickly and secretly writing the number down.

Martin phoned the number and was given an appointment for the following week. Six months on, Martin went to the pub for a drink in the early evening. Many of his friends' thought he had been away.

He started to laugh with them and realised how he had shut himself away for so long because he had been terrified to leave his house. Slowly, he started to socialise again and stopped missing work. He was lucky that he didn't lose his job altogether. What had changed him was that he had been given a unique opportunity to talk about his experience in confidence and to be believed and listened to without judgement. Martin never told his friends about what had happened nor did he ever report it to the police.

Georgina

'Georgina are you ready?' shouted her mother up the stairs. 'Beth and Jenny are here.' Georgina didn't go out much since splitting up with her boyfriend. 'I'm quite looking forward to this,' she said, as she glided down the stairs in her new outfit.

Two hours later the girls were laughing, joking and generally catching up in the Old Black Pig pub. Georgina was beautiful, and it was not long before she attracted the attention of a man who had been looking across at the three friends for some time.

'Can I buy you a drink, love?' The man's eye contact with the barman seemed to say that they were friends.

'No thanks, this is a girl's night out only, no men allowed.'

Georgina woke up staring at the night sky. All she knew was that she could smell wet grass and that she seemed to be alone. Her mind was racing. Was she dead? She could feel pain rippling throughout her body and her head was bleeding. She couldn't be dead, could she? She started to get up. Although she was very dizzy, she groped her way to a wooden bench and realised from somewhere in the depths of her subconscious and memory, that she must be in a park or field.

Through blurred and hazy vision, she managed to get to a road and walked out as she saw a passing car...

It was two days later when Georgina woke up with eyes looking down at her. They belonged to the familiar faces of her mother and sister.

'Where am I, what happened to me?'

'We'd like to know the answer to that too, Georgie,' said her mum. Georgina was in the local hospital. She had been transferred there from two cities away. Having no idea how she came to be there or what had happened to her in the lapsed time was of great concern to her, her family and the police. So many questions entered her head: What happened to me? Was I raped? By how many people? What happened to my friends? Why do I hurt so much? Are there photographs?

The passage of time for which there was no remembered information heightened Georgina's anxiety and fear. There was medical evidence to confirm that she had in fact been the victim of a gang rape. DNA samples had been collected and a long wait now ensued for her as the police endeavoured to catch the perpetrators.

The forensic chemical tests carried out on Georgina after the attack showed traces of Ketamine in her system. Ketamine is a short-acting general anaesthetic that has hallucinogenic and painkilling qualities that seem to affect people in very different ways. Some people describe a speedy rush within a few minutes of sniffing the powder (20 minutes if taken as a pill, quicker if injected), leading to powerful hallucinations and even out of body experiences (the 'K-hole'), along with physical incapacitation.

If on a dance floor, music can sound heavy, weird and strangely compelling, lights seem very intense and physical coordination can fall apart along with an overall feeling of numbness. Some people feel paralysed by the drug, unable to speak without slurring, while others either feel sick or vomit.

As this crime has become more prevalent so indeed has the preventative industry and several anti-drink spiking items are now available such as bottle top stoppers, which work by popping into the neck of a bottle to thwart substances being put in the drink. There is also Drink Detectives, a drink testing kit, developed to ascertain if a drink has been tampered with. Although these are great ideas and send a message that action is in place to safeguard us, unfortunately the sexual predators continue to find ways to render them ineffective.

Kevin

At 34 Kevin had had many girlfriends. They had come and gone. 'Like they do,' he used to say. He was happy with his life as a marketing manager in London. Tracey, his latest girlfriend, was due to meet him in the Blue Orchid bar. Eight o'clock came and went, and there was still no sign of Tracey. Kevin had downed at least four pints of lager and was starting to feel the effects. The nightclub was heaving, and it always amazed him how he rarely saw the same crowd twice when he went there.

He tried ringing Tracey a few times, but he got no answer and guessed he must have been stood up. Oh well, another one bites the dust, he thought! A few lads came in and sat down around the bar. They got chatting about women and how they always let you down in the end and had a good laugh about how many times they had each been stood up. One of the lads called John seemed to be the leader of the others, and he insisted on buying the drinks all night – Kevin guessed he must be their boss, so he enjoyed their company and accepted the drinks happily.

It was cold and just starting to get light when Kevin started to come round; he was on waste ground and in a lot of pain. He soon realised that he was completely undressed from the waist down. He was violently sick and realised to his horror he had been raped but had no recollection of it, just hazy flashbacks. He must have been really drunk, he thought. Something told him to get to the police station. He found his clothes scattered around and carefully got up. Somehow he made it to the police station, and luckily for him the desk sergeant was very understanding, obviously being experienced in this area.

He took Kevin straight into an interview room, and there he waited to make a statement. He was taken immediately to the nearest victim suite and given a full forensic medical examination. He was also given some different clothes, as the police needed to keep his own for forensic evidence purposes. After he had given his statement, which was videoed throughout, he was taken home. He was handed a leaflet at the police station for a local rape crisis centre and also a helpline number, which offered help for men who have been sexually assaulted.

A man was caught and arrested on the DNA evidence found at the scene, and the case went to Crown Court. The man who was the 'boss' from the Blue Orchid pub was identified as the rapist and given a four-year prison sentence.

Margaret

Margaret was six years old when her father first took her into his bed. She remembers thinking it was a game, and she was giggling. It started with tickling, and she related how shock and silence took over, how her body went rigid, as he did things to her she didn't understand.

Over the next four years her father systematically raped and used her body in all kinds of degrading ways. Her mother worked at the local supermarket and often worked long hours. He had told Margaret that if she ever spoke about their 'special times' he would kill her mother, just like he did the pigs and chickens for their Sunday roasts. Children have no choice but to submit to abuse especially when threatened with the death of a loved one.

Margaret learned very quickly to remove herself from her body and from the situation. She stated that she often saw herself being abused as if looking down from above and hovering at ceiling level.

This process has many names, one of which is dissociation (or detachment), which simplified means creatively shutting off reality in order to survive the traumatic event taking place in the here and now.

When she was ten years old, Margaret's father was found dead in his car in his garage with the exhaust carefully fitted to make it a quick suicide. This is what ultimately stopped the sexual abuse.

Margaret says she was in shock for some months and completely blamed herself for his death, as did her mother. During the abuse he had continually told her that she was 'special and that he loved her'. She loved him or at least thought this was how she was meant to love and be loved. Margaret's mother, Christine, was always sick of her and blamed her for killing her husband, until Christine met Frank.

Margaret was immediately afraid of him, and he would grab her for 'special cuddles' when her mum was out of sight. For the next three years Frank took over where her father left off, and Margaret told me that she actually believed this was what she was supposed to do. This was what all men did and that girls were supposed to be used in secret in this way.

In fact, her belief was so strong that one day when she was 13, she was having Sunday dinner with her mum, Frank, grandma and grandfather and she inadvertently told them all how well she was doing at school and how she had always done what the men had told her to do so she would one day become a good wife, not only in the kitchen but also in the bedroom.

Her grandfather immediately reacted to this, choking on a mouthful of his dinner and asking her what she meant, and as Frank began to turn more and more crimson, Margaret realised that she had said something she shouldn't have. Her mother slapped her across the face, calling her a little slut, and told her to go to her room, but her grandfather quickly intercepted this and took her outside to ask her what she meant.

He was kind, not like the other men she knew. Her Grandad was her best friend in the world. She smiled as she related this liberating day. She remembered that she also loved him in a different way to her father. He sat her down and told the others to keep out whilst he talked to her. While this was going on Frank got to his feet and slowly left out of the front door.

For the next hour Margaret sobbed and sobbed as she told her grandfather everything about Frank and how she thought it was alright, because she could leave her body, and it was always over quickly, not like when Daddy used to do it. At this her grandfather sunk his head in his hands, kissed her head and told her he would be back in a minute. Margaret was terrified and thought she was in so much trouble. She wanted to bolt, but something inside her trusted her Grandad and just hoped he would not be bringing her mother out to slap her again.

Half an hour or so later, the police came and talked to Margaret for a while; they asked if she'd like to make a video saying the things she'd already said but in more detail. Grandad went with her, and she felt safe.

So, in her early teens Margaret welcomed a move to live with her grandparents and then later went on to university. No one ever spoke about the abuse, and she quietly 'put it away'. The police were unable to locate Frank and her father was dead, so there was no case and no conviction.

Margaret excelled at university and finally got her degree in child psychology at the age of 21. Her grandparents' health was deteriorating, and she went home to take care of them both whilst looking for a position at a children's hospital. At 35, Margaret got married. She had gone through much with the death of her mother and both grandparents, and now she was married to one of the doctors at the hospital, and they began a harmonious life together in a beautiful house with everything she could ever dream of.

Two years later Margaret was due to give birth to a son, whom she named Alfie after her grandfather, Alfred. After the birth she became very depressed and almost unable to function. The doctors, and especially her husband, put it down to postnatal depression, and he hired a nanny to take care of Alfie.

Still struggling to come to terms with flashbacks from her childhood and intrusive thoughts, Margaret engaged in therapy.

After some initial rapport building and relating of her experience we were able to work through her historic life path and how her reaction now was a trigger, a connection to those past experiences. Triggers are an experience of overwhelming feelings, sensations and impulses: not only of 'I was in danger then' but '*I am in danger now*'.

After hearing her story the counsellor could see that Margaret was suffering from emotional, physical, physiological trauma commonly known as RR-PTSD. After ten weeks of intense therapy, post-trauma intervention and much investment on Margaret's part she was able to start to understand some of the abuse, her current reactions and how she could move on from what had happened by lessening the impact of the abuse. What impressed her most was her sudden reconnection with Alfie, her son, who up until this point she had not bonded with properly.

I received an email from Margaret a while ago, and she told me she rarely if ever thinks about the bad times in the 'Wild Wood', as she called it; she now lives a fulfilling life and has three happy and well-adjusted children. She said she feels valued as a mother and a wife but most of all as a person in her own right.

In a never-ending cycle of abuse her father fulfilled his twisted fantasy by actually acting it out. This then magnified the fantasy effect, causing him to seek to further satisfy his depravation repeatedly on his daughter. In keeping her silent he was able to ensure continued access, guaranteeing silence and the power to further abuse. When a child who has been sexually violated moves on into adulthood, the fact that the physical/sexual touching and assaults have stopped can seem like the end.

On reflection in later life, victims look back at their abuse with the eyes of an adult and not the terror of a vulnerable child. It can often be too late to seek justice against the perpetrator, but it is never too late to start to heal and with the right help this can be achieved. It takes a huge amount of courage for those targeted by paedophiles to finally find a voice and speak out against those who have molested them.

Adam

Adam came into therapy after having had palpitations at work. He couldn't work out why he was feeling so anxious all the time. We went through his history, and he told me he grew up in a family of six – four boys and two girls – and that he was second from youngest.

We worked with a time line to start with and sketched out a life journey from birth to his present age. He worked well in filling in the gaps for me so that I had a good understanding of his journey so far. From 9 to 11 years old his brother Ethan told him that sex was supposed to be with boys first and then later on with girls. His brother had promised him that if he would just do as he was told now, then he would help him get a girl when the time was right for him.

Ethan was 18 at the time, legally a grown man, and took advantage of his brother on a weekly, sometimes daily, basis. Adam stated that the only saving grace for him was that because there were so many in the family, it was not often he was trapped alone with Ethan.

When he was alone with his brother, Ethan expected Adam to agree to sex if he groped his genitals or bottom as he was doing his chores. Adam grew to hate Ethan and knew deep inside that this was all wrong somehow. It was painful and just not right. He told Ethan how he felt, but he just said that it wasn't normal behaviour for a young boy not to do it. If he didn't carry on he would be known as a freak at school and all of his friends would know and laugh at him. He was so young, so naïve, he believed he was a freak; he believed Ethan and he felt ashamed of himself for reacting in this way.

Reflecting later on that Boxing Day holiday, Adam wished he had gone to walk the dogs with the rest of his family, because what happened next changed the course of his life in many ways. He didn't know it at the time, but Ethan was at home too. After groping at him and being rebuked, Ethan pinned Adam down and forced himself on him. Adam felt so sick he begged and pleaded with him to stop. He did not have the physical strength to stop him. His brother, once his hero, was buggering him.

Ethan justified it by saying that he could not control himself. He said it wasn't his fault. Then he told Adam that their father had sexually abused him as a young boy. Adam was a sensitive child and empathised with him. He pitied him for his past abuse. And Ethan, in that moment, successfully made Adam consider himself a wimp and a freak. Ethan was the real victim wasn't he? Adam's mind was in chaos.

Ethan forced himself upon Adam whenever he got the chance. Adam would pray it would end quickly. All of a sudden when he was around 11 the sexual abuse just stopped.

What he remembered most from those dark days was a morning in July; he remembered that because all the windows were open and the house was unusually bright. He walked past his brother Nigel's bedroom and saw him crying on the side of his bed. He went in to see what was wrong and to put his hand on his shoulder and Nigel flinched away. The conversation went something like this:

Adam: What's wrong mate?

Nigel: I can't tell you. Go away. I fucking hate you.

Adam: Just tell me Nige. Is it Ethan? Is he hurting you?

There was a long pause as both brothers looked into each other's eyes, waiting – Adam needing to know and Nigel desperately wanting to answer.

Adam: Just tell me Nige, please, I can help you.

Nigel: You can't stop it. You're the one who started it all.

Adam: No, no, I'm not, Nige. It was Ethan, he started on me a couple of years ago, he told me that it had to be like this, that we would never get girls unless we did it with a boy first.

Nigel cried long sobs and fell to his knees.

Nigel: That's exactly what he told me, Addie.

They both got out of the house and just ran and ran until they couldn't run any more and ended up at Tilde's (the woman who ran the youth club) house. Praying that she would be in, they knocked and got a short sharp mouthful from her, and then an invitation on to the garden for squash and a chat.

The brothers told Tilde what had been happening. Tilde wasted no time in calling the authorities and their parents. In this case, after a long process whereby all boys had to continue to live in the same house, Ethan was sent to Crown Court and convicted of rape, buggery and offences against a child on 27 counts that he pleaded guilty to. There was huge unrest in the family, not least because Adam felt he had to question his own father about Ethan's claims of abuse at his hands, which his father vehemently denied and said made him feel sick to the stomach. In the counselling session Adam could not think why he had suddenly started to feel anxious. He had been having panic attacks and was spending a lot of time crying for what he described as 'no apparent reason'. I asked if there had been any changes recently or events in his life that were either new or unfamiliar to him.

Adam thought for a moment and slapped his forehead with both hands. 'How could I have been so stupid?' he said. It turned out that a new employee had started at the call centre where he worked who bore a striking resemblance to his oldest brother, Ethan.

On asking him when the anxiety had started he related the incident when he went out to the toilet, and this new employee followed him – not for any sinister reason, just to use the toilet. The trigger responses that he experienced caused his amygdala – the reptilian part of his brain to make him acutely aware of the recognition face template of his brother and the similarity of this new employee, causing his body to react in exactly the same way as it did when he was a child being abused by Ethan.

We worked for ten weeks using a combination of Eye Movement Desensitisation Reprocessing (EMDR) and Brain Spotting (BSP) intervention together with various self-soothing techniques in order to assist Adam with his present reaction and also future reactions.

The long-term effects of childhood sexual abuse can be described as being like sunburn. At the time the physical pain can be unbearable but after some time, the sunburn and discolouration subside and the evidence of the burn disappears. However, the long-term damage to the skin goes far deeper and these effects may not come out for some time.

Marcus

At age 47 Marcus came to counselling after experiencing intermittent flashbacks and vague recollections of 'something', though he seemed to be unaware of where these thoughts and images came from and did not know what they were. After much exploration through floods of tears and great distress Marcus disclosed, vaguely at first, how when he was six years old his two brothers would get him to come and play in the hayloft, 'their den', where once he was up they would pull up the ladder and make him take his clothes off, coercing him to perform oral sex on each of them in turn. At other times it would be anal sex and each would bugger him in turn, telling him that this was normal for boys, and he must do it or one of their mother's boyfriends would kick him to death, just as they had all witnessed him do to a stray dog recently.

Such was the effect of this conditioning and brainwashing and his trust and belief in what they had threatened, that Marcus had never told a single living soul until he came into therapy under the guise of relationship issues. It had taken well over eight sessions before he felt able to disclose anything at all about the abuse.

Marcus had survived throughout his adolescence and adulthood this far because he had very quickly learned to adjust to his environment in an effort to survive (also known as creative adjustment) and to dissociate from reality (a psychological defence mechanism in which specific, anxiety-provoking thoughts, emotions or physical sensations are separated from the rest of the psyche).

As life took hold, with new experiences, work and relationships of his own, Marcus distanced himself far away from his toxic brothers and his emotionally absent mother, changed his name and his identity and continued to live his life shrouded in shame nd secrecy. Those who knew him often wondered if he was okay as he was so quiet, and his wife Scarlet sometimes remarked that she thought he must be clinically depressed to be so quiet and 'shut off' about his family, because he would never tell her anything about them. One day after a more serious argument she said: 'If you don't start telling me the truth about you and your family, I'm leaving. I deserve to know the truth.'

Through complex post-trauma intervention of EMDR over 24 therapeutic sessions, where sometimes the whole 90 minutes would be taken up with Marcus's sheer distressing abreactions at the reality of his past, he was slowly able to process the abuse his brothers had systematically perpetrated upon him as a child. He became able to let go of what he called the 'real dirt' and could talk more freely as well as make some positive choices about his life and his future.

At his request I agreed for him to bring his wife to one session, where he felt safer and more able to disclose the childhood abuse and the reasons why he had felt it necessary to change his identity. His wife found this difficult to comprehend and later found it useful to have some counselling sessions herself with another therapist.

We recently had an email from Marcus and Scarlet who have just had a baby girl. They have now moved abroad and are happy and settled into their new life.

Donna

Alan and Donna were eight years apart in age. When Alan was 15 and Donna was seven years old, he started to teach her how to dance and play new games. He bought her comics and toys and he was her 'hero'. Their parents, Marjorie and Del, were so proud of their two children and the special relationship they seemed to have. They loved how Alan protected and looked after his sister.

It wasn't until Donna was nearly nine years old that something in the sibling relationship started to change. Later, during counselling, Donna was able to recall and could almost pinpoint the exact moment and day that her brother changed towards her. It was immediately after her ninth birthday, and she had just had a great birthday party outside in the garden.

Marjorie and Del had been invited next door for a drink with the 'grown ups', and Alan and Donna had been told to get cleaned up for their tea later.

Alan started to show Donna a new dance he said he'd learnt at school. Donna's recollection of this dance was that it felt weird and made her giggle in equal measure, but it unsettled her; over time the dances required less and less clothing until somehow, almost like magic she thought, they would both be completely naked.

Alan had been grooming his little sister over years with perfect sibling behaviour and so-called brotherly love. He began to replace previous comics with pornographic material, slowly sexualising her and normalising the behaviour so that she submitted to sexual behaviour, which included him raping her on a daily basis. When she said 'no', which was every time, he would use force and threats to get his way.

Donna recalled that the worse type of coercion was when he would cry that he had no friends and how she was making him worse by not just doing as she was told. This made her feel terrible, and in an effort not to hurt him further, she would give in to make him happy, as she could not bear for her once hero of a brother to be sad. Alan used her love to get his needs met.

The sibling sexual violation continued for five years and was made even worse for Donna after their parents had another child who took up all of their time, leaving the care of Donna up to Alan most of the time. When Donna was 14 the abuse finally stopped because Alan left home to join the Metropolitan Police Force in London.

While Alan's career rocketed over the years, Donna's life slowly plummeted further and further down into spiralling misery. She failed desperately at school, leaving her parents disappointed and unhappy with her.

Their 'assumed' rationale for this behaviour was that she must be 'missing' her brother. If only they knew! Many years later

Donna's fortieth birthday arrived, and her family held a surprise party for her. All family and extended family were invited, including Alan, his wife Cherry and their two daughters Ellie and Gemma, five and eight years old.

Donna managed to hold it together until her brother asked her to dance. This struck fear into her heart and she started to experience a panic attack, so severe that an ambulance was called for a suspected heart attack.

As Donna was kept in, it was in the silence and stillness of the hospital in the middle of the night that she found the courage to tell her husband Robert exactly what had happened to her during her lost childhood. For Robert this answered so many questions in his own head, including her reluctance to have sex. Intimacy was almost banned between them. If she saw her children or other siblings playing too closely, she would question it. It was like a revelation and an annihilating blow to him all at the same time.

Robert, ever the loving and protective husband, was red with anger. As tears filled his eyes, he kissed her forehead and left her to sleep. In the following days Donna was allowed home after observations at the hospital were complete. As she recovered, Robert took over. He spoke to her parents and organised an initial counselling assessment to give her much-needed space and time. She clearly needed to talk and disclose the complex level of her childhood trauma that now overwhelmed her.

It was at Donna's insistence that the police were not involved. However, anonymous letters were sent to all parties concerned with her nieces such as social services, schools and the child protection unit of the police force near to where Alan worked. Whether those letters were ever used or not, the real surprise to this story came when the elder of her two nieces attended an emotional outlet 'Pow-wow' meeting at her school one Tuesday morning. A friend of Gemma's, Jenny, who had recently been to their house to play, said very loudly at the meeting when it was her turn to speak: 'Gemma's daddy has been tickling me on my front bottom, and I've been touching him on his. It's a new game – we can all play it.'

At this point all relevant multi-agency parties were called in: social services, child protection police section and school SENCO personnel. Gemma and Ellie were questioned, as was the friend, and after a long process Alan was eventually taken to court. He was never imprisoned but was put on the Sex Offenders Register.

This gave Donna the courage to tell her parents the truth about her childhood. They were shocked and full of disbelief and did not talk to her for many years. After some reconciliation instigated by Robert they made their peace, and Donna forgave her parents for disbelieving her, as they in turn acknowledged her pain, suffering and loss. This was a long and winding road for Donna and one she never envisaged walking.

Thankfully, Donna had Robert who, with her consent, helped her in every way possible to work through some of the darkest times. He was able to stand up for her, stand by her and stand in between her and anyone who might hurt her.

Jane

Jane, a single mother of three, worked hard at her local supermarket. Three years previously her husband, Jonathan, had been killed in action in Afghanistan. She was still grieving but was seen outwardly as 'getting on with it' for the kids' sake.

Jane had been left comfortably off. With her widow's and army pension together with the wages she took home from her job, she was able to keep herself and the three children in food and clothes. They often were able to afford little holidays and the latest gear.

The children kept her sanity at a pretty high level most of the time, and they spent the odd weekend just remembering Jonathan, talking, laughing and crying about him until they had spent their emotion for that weekend. The youngest boy, Edward, was never able to talk about his Dad and preferred just to listen to the others.

The children each had their own computers in their room, and their online time was carefully balanced between schoolwork, housework, sports, family time and friends. Weekends and holidays allowed for extra time online, as did doing extra chores around the house.

As well as computers each of the children had their own iPod, MP3 players and the latest mobile phones.

Joshua 13 (Josh)

Josh, the studious one, the bookworm, always completed his homework before anyone else. He loved school, studying and the internet. From an early age Josh had been able to build a simple website and was always on hand to help his friends with their homework or latest technical problem. He had 118 friends on Facebook.

Olivia 12 (Livvy)

Livvy had lots of friends, was very pretty and loved pink things. She knew her way around a computer but used it mostly for Facebooking and meeting friends with whom she spent most of her time. She had 246 friends on Facebook.

Edward 10 (Eds)

Eds hated computers except for games – especially computer cricket games. Eds spent nearly all of his time playing cricket, the game his Dad taught him to play. He had 89 friends on Facebook.

Recently Eds had a new friend on Facebook, a friend called Jake. They had been messaging each other for about two months, and all they ever messaged about was cricket, cricket, cricket!

One day the conversation turned to Eds' dad and how he felt about his death. Eds had never been able to talk properly about his feelings before. He just put all his grieving energy into playing cricket, fully believing that his Dad was watching him from a star – a star that his Grandma pointed to on the night of his Dad's funeral telling him that his Dad was there forever watching over him. Jake seemed to be the only person he could really talk to, who could understand his loss. Jake said his Dad had died too in Afghanistan and that he had lost his best friend. He said he was completely lost without him.

Eds loved this. He loved having an outlet for his delayed grief, someone to talk to who didn't judge him or tell him what to do, and someone who just listened. Soon everyone around started to notice how happy he had become. Jake had warned Eds that he would only upset everyone if he told them he'd been talking about his Dad, so he never told anyone and continued to enjoy his newfound friendship. They had exchanged photos, and Eds thought he and Jake even looked alike.

Jake had been saying it was time they met up, so they could really talk about their lives and dreams for their future. They both wanted to be pilots in the Royal Air Force.

Now Josh, who was a bit of computer geek, had noticed Eds' extra time on the internet and thought that he must have a girlfriend, so he decided for fun to hack into his brother's Facebook account. Getting this sort of information would be of great benefit, should he need him to do his housework share at some time and even just to tease and/or bribe him would be cool.

What Josh found made him stop in his tracks; he felt weird, and he didn't like the way the feed had been going. He felt a sense of dread when he saw Eds and Jake were planning to meet up the following Thursday after school at the park not too far away.

Josh spoke to Livvy, who abruptly told him to 'mind his own business and let Eds get on with his life', but when he showed her the message feed, she said she felt weird too and worried about her younger brother. They had all been warned about the dangers on the internet, but Eds probably hadn't taken any notice or even thought this could be a potential risk.

They decided to tell their mum, and when Jane arrived home, they commandeered her into the front lounge out of earshot of Eds, who was out in the garden practising his batting. They told Jane how worried they felt, and just to be on the safe side Jane rang her friend, Polly, whose husband was a police officer. He came round with Polly for a cup of tea, while Livvy and Josh took Eds to the youth café.

Eds did meet Jake at the park on the following Thursday after school, and Jake turned out to be 43 years old and a convicted sex offender, whose victim group just happened to be young boys. Fortunately for Eds, Jane and the Internet Police Investigation Team also met Jake at the park.

Jake, aka Richard Green, was later convicted under the Sex Offences Act 2004 – Schedule 3 = 24 'An offence under section 15 of this Act (meeting a child following sexual grooming)'. He was sentenced to 16 months in prison with a five-year listing on the Sex Offenders Register.

Jake

Meg and John were Jake's parents. After a long hard week at the sandwich shop they owned, they would be tired and worn out. Every Saturday night it would be the same scenario. They would go to the pub, get very drunk, come home, and a fight between them would break out. John would always win, and Meg would wake up covered in bruises.

Jake would sit at the top of the stairs listening, terrified that one day one of them would kill the other. He was 12 now and was often left in the house on his own, where he liked to sit in his room painting and drawing.

As an adult in counselling he related how, ironically, his parents would never let him have a television in his room because of the violence. He remembers wishing that his dad would just leave. Then he and his mum could have some peace and happiness again like they used to before they bought that stupid shop, which just made them grumpy all of the time making him feel left out, isolated and lonely. It was as if they didn't notice him any more, and they were both gone all day and most evenings working.

Jake spent a lot of his time walking or cycling to different places where he would get out his sketchpad and draw anything that took his eye; he was particularly good at landscapes so the higher he could get, the better, for his special view.

He met many people on his trips out. He could stay out all day and all night, and no one would notice if he was missing.

In one of the shops near to his home he would often stop and talk to Eddie, the newsagent. He was a nice bloke and often gave Jake an extra comic, if he had any left from the unsold last issues. He would ask Jake questions about his 'lovely mother'.

'How is she? I haven't seen her around for ages.' This made Jake laugh, as he knew that his Mum had a bit of a 'thing' for Eddie, as this was often the main topic of his parent's weekend arguments.

It was the summer holidays, and Jake was let free as usual to do his drawing and painting, but now he had a shiny new camera that Eddie had given him.' Well, I don't use it any more. You may as well get some use out of it, son.'

On hearing about this fantastic 'gift', Meg had offered to pay Eddie for the camera, but he wouldn't hear of it, although he did say: 'You can always come out for dinner with me if you like.'

The relationship between Eddie and Meg progressed, as John got further and further into drinking and gambling and was not only away from home a lot of the time but also away from the sandwich bar, which left Meg to handle things on her own. Jake was called in to help and to earn some extra cash to buy his much loved art equipment and proper film for his camera.

It wasn't long before Eddie and Meg became an item. Meg and Jake moved into his big house just up the road, leaving John to wallow in his gambling debts, drink and self-pity as his life went pretty much downhill. Life was so much better for Jake as he started at his new school and made new friends and seemed happy with his lot.

That was until one Bank Holiday morning when his mother had left for work. She had long since sold the sandwich bar and was now working for Eddie in his news agency.

'Your Mum tells me you'd like to learn fly fishing. Is that right, Jake?'

'Yes, Eddie I'd love it. When can we go?'

'Well, we can go today, if you're up for it. Let's get ready. I know a great place.'

Jake remembers that it was so exciting, sitting in the car with Eddie and all his fishing gear. His Dad had never taken him fishing.

If he was honest he did sometimes feel a little bit uncomfortable around Eddie and didn't like the way he looked at him at times, but that was so much better than the violence with his Mum and Dad that he'd previously experienced every weekend.

They got to the fishing lakes, and Jake was ready to just start anywhere at any old lake, but Eddie insisted the fish were more plentiful on the farthest lakeside, so they carried all the gear over there. They got the fishing gear set up, donned the feathered hats that fly fishermen wear and were having a good laugh. It was at this point that Jake asked Eddie how to do it properly.

As Eddie showed him the fishing rod, he came up behind him very close, moved his arms around Jake to show him how to achieve the fly motion, and Jake could feel him up close.

That day Eddie sexually abused Jake on the bank of the isolated fishing lake, and he told him that he now belonged to him to do exactly as he said and that if he even thought about telling his mother or father that they would send him away for lying, that they didn't really care anyway.

Through deep sobs and big tears, Jake told me that he had always thought he'd got what he wished for and could never tell a living soul; how could he put his mother through that after what she had already been through? He was 47 when he came to Jigsaw Post Trauma and Counselling Services and had kept his 'secret' for over 30 years. He stated that luckily for him, Eddie died a year after they moved into his house and the abuse obviously stopped.

After Eddie's death, Jake really believed that he could put it away somewhere in a box in his head and forget it. He had an accident at work as a scaffolding leader and was knocked unconscious by one of the falling scaffold poles. When he awoke, all he could think about was the abuse he suffered as a child and he needed desperately to talk it through, to let it out. After three months of intensive inner-child work and letting-go intervention, Jake was able to reduce the frequency of his weekly sessions to fortnightly and then gradually these decreased to monthly sessions.

In that time he had made a choice to look into other areas of building work and years later qualified as a building surveyor.

Jake kept in touch and now has a high-powered job, two more children and is settled with his wife of 18 years. He states that he feels he has finally let go of his inner scream and torment.

As you can see from this case history, Eddie's sole intention for instigating a relationship with Meg was so that he could abuse her son. The grooming took him a while, but once he knew he had full control and power over Jake, he used it to his full advantage to both exploit him and gratify his own sexual needs as the paedophile he was.

Helen

'Why don't you ever do as you are told?' Helen's mum was shouting at her to hurry up as usual.

'Now get yourself ready properly. Have you brushed your teeth yet? I have to drop you next door in a minute, otherwise we won't have any money for food, if I don't get out to work.' Helen was still crying as her mum was shaking her. She remembers being about five or six, and it was the beginning of the six weeks of school holidays.

Lydia, Helen's mother, had not been in Halyard Close long before the neighbours had offered her their hand of friendship, often bringing cakes and goodies for the single mum and her little daughter.

Helen hated going next door to the Latimers' house. They were so horrible to her and made her do 'secret' things while she was playing with her dolls or colouring at the table.

Mr Latimer would sit her on his lap and get her to bounce up and down while he made funny noises and his wife watched from the door. This wasn't fun. It was strange. She liked it in a way, but it took a lot for her to understand the reasons behind those feelings. (Our genitalia, when caressed in certain ways, are designed to make us feel good. As children we have no schema for whether it is right or wrong; our bodies get confused.)

Whatever Mr Latimer did with Helen, it was never as bad as what Mrs Latimer did to her. She was ordered to call her Ma'am and to do as she was told at all times. Sometimes Mrs Latimer would hit her with a light plastic strap across her bare bottom leaving no marks. She had a knack of doing so, and at other times she would be ordered to do things to gratify Mrs Latimer.

The threats that both Mr and Mrs Latimer used were that 'big girls *do not cry*' and that they would kill her Mum, but before they killed her they would stick hatpins in her eyes so that she cried blood before she died.

They would show her the long sharp hatpins, which would be brought out at regular intervals during the abuse, if she even hesitated to do what she was told by Mrs Latimer. As a child, she was constantly terrified and would 'act up' every time she had to go next door. Her mother asked her time and time again what was wrong. Why didn't she want to go next door? After all they were lovely people, so kind, and she should be grateful to them for having her. Helen would look into her Mum's eyes to see their beautiful green colour. She couldn't bear the thought of big pins sticking out of them, so she kept quiet and learnt how to deal with it, how to 'creatively adjust' in order to survive.

After the summer holidays, Helen went back to school. The Latimers moved house, and the abuse stopped just as quickly as it had started. She was so happy not to have to go there again. School with all its rules and regulations was a piece of cake to her compared with what she had previously endured.

The years rolled by. Helen sailed through school and later university. She attained excellent marks in everything she did. She got married and three years later she gave birth to her daughter, Angelina. In counselling, Helen stated that everything changed for her from the very moment she gave birth to her daughter. To her, it was as if all the studying and hard work she had used over the years to hide the abuse had been pointless, because now it all came flooding back as she held her tiny 6lb 4oz daughter in her arms.

Helen refused to go out. She became so protective over this little bundle that home life became unbearable, almost intolerable for her husband.

She wouldn't allow any of her family or her husband's family to hold the baby, and if they did, she would be watching their every move. It was suggested by a family friend, a GP, that she look into a talking therapy or similar to assist with her reaction.

Helen stated that she actually found counselling a refreshing place to be, where she felt free to talk about everything and get it all out in the open safely and confidentially. Helen related that the way she had coped over the years was to dissociate. Once she got pregnant, and particularly later in the pregnancy, her hormones and her maternal instinct overwhelmed her, leaving her unable to use the dissociative coping method that she had previously relied upon.

Helen had many months of counselling, and the disclosures she made were difficult because her mother was still alive, and the threat of her seeing those hatpins sticking out of the still beautiful but ageing green eyes filled her with dread.

Initially, triggers for her were immense and often looked upon by others as a bit weird. For example, she had not been able to be near anyone who wore a hat or go into an antique shop or department stores where they sold either hats or anything resembling a hatpin.

Helen left counselling with a positive and new outlook. She has three more children now, so has her work cut out as a full-time mum. A couple of years ago I received a gift from her in the post at Christmas 2010; it was a hatpin attached to a card that read: 'I will never be able to thank you enough.'

Varsha

Before I went through the critical incident debrief therapy, I was slightly dubious as to whether it would work and also how it worked! The process took two hours and required me to talk through my traumatic experience in as much factual detail as I could remember. The therapist encouraged the use of deep breathing techniques, so that I was able to remain calm. The second part of the therapy involved my expression of the feeling and emotions experienced at the time of the rape.

The whole session was a simple and very positive experience. Afterwards I had a feeling of elation, which was in contrast to how I felt before the debriefing. The weight had been lifted from my shoulders.

Although I can obviously remember all the details of the traumatic attack, they are no longer a constant thought in my head. I think of it only if I choose to, and it is no longer something which causes me pain, unhappiness or stops me from working.

What I had initially feared would undermine my whole future feels firmly in the past, and I now have the confidence and strength to move forward with my life and career.

Laura

Laura lived in a cul-de-sac. Her property has a walled garden, and the back entrance is from the road via a wrought iron gate to the side. She loved her house, her garden and her two cats and had many friends and neighbours who she loved to visit.

One morning in June, Laura let one of her cats out into the garden and left the back door slightly ajar in order for it to come back in.

In those split seconds an intruder came into her kitchen and unleashed a savage attack on Laura before raping her and then kicking her continuously with such force that she lost consciousness. There she lay until a neighbour who had seen a man running out of the side gate came in to see what was going on.

Laura spent 12 weeks in hospital, four of those in intensive care, and underwent surgery with a further two months in convalescence. By the time she was referred to me eight months later, she had attempted suicide three times. She had turned to alcohol and drugs in an attempt to obliterate the reality of her experience, and several body symptoms such as arthritis and psoriasis had manifested her mental state.

After hearing her story, I could see that Laura was suffering from emotional, physical and physiological trauma. Shock and trauma go right to the very core of our existence and to be able to remove this from a person's psyche can be likened to taking a splinter from deep beneath the skin.

Doctors, nurses, psychiatrists, health professionals, psychologists and psychotherapists all play their part in trying to assist a traumatised individual. However, sometimes they fail to see the splinter.

After six or seven counselling sessions it became apparent that counselling was not working for Laura, and that in order for her to benefit, she needed to somehow lessen the impact that the vicious attack had left with her. I explained the process of psychological debriefing and the way I had been taught; I explained that it was not counselling. Laura said she was prepared to try anything, and I have to say that at this point I had my own doubts of its effectiveness. This was mainly because of the injuries she had sustained, one of which had resulted in having a metal plate inserted into her head.

The following week I carried out the psychological debrief, which took two and a quarter hours. We booked a further appointment for four weeks later, and Laura went home.

On that fourth week, I opened the door to Laura who seemed to have changed her appearance somehow. I asked her how she'd been – a smile came over her face and lit up her eyes (something I had not seen happen before). She said, 'I don't know what you did or how you did it, but it's worked. I don't want to die any more, and I've decided to start to make a new life for myself. I've already decided to do some voluntary work in one of the charity shops in the town. For the first time since the attack I put my own rubbish out last week. I now have extra security but I don't think about dying any more.'

Laura was left for dead in an unprovoked attack, leaving her world in utter chaos for many months. Before the psychological debrief she had totally isolated herself in the newly secured safety of her own home, the very place where the attack had taken place. She had been unable to leave her house or have interpersonal relationships even with her own family.

As a direct result of the psychological debrief session Laura was able to start to revive her life and carry out normal everyday tasks.

Malcolm

At first I went for some sessions of EMDR after reading about it on the internet; the therapist explained how it worked. I answered the questions and did the eye thing as and when I was asked. The issue I had taken was seeing my friend's body after he had committed suicide; I had never been able to get the image out of my mind. A few months before, he had told me how four men had raped him after a night out. On reflection now, I realise he never really got over it and never sought any help.

The therapist asked me things like what was the worst part of the image I held in my mind. She asked me to describe images and scale certain answers from one to seven or one to ten. I initially wondered what this was all about, but after the first session I soon began to realise that my scaled answers and the impact of them had already become less, and it had somehow desensitised my feelings and reactions to the image I had previously of my friend's lifeless body. Altogether I had seven sessions of EMDR, and throughout those weeks my mind seemed to bring things up that I had not thought about in a long time, and each one seemed to make sense of the other.

I now feel happy and as if a weight has been lifted from my shoulders, a weight I have carried for a very long time. I still live with the regret that my friend did not seek this help for himself and wonder if he even knew such help was available.

Kristiana

When I was 14, I was raped by my brother's friend. He came to our house to see my brother who wasn't in at 5pm, so I said he could wait.

This friend knew our family and that our parents never got home until about 8pm, as they had their own newsagent business. Later on I realised he also knew that my brother would be out at football practice till 8pm. This had been a planned attack, one that I never told anyone about until I was 32, because at the time he had threatened to kill my brother in an 'accident' if I told anyone. He said he would 'see to it' that he would die, and it would be my fault.

After the rape I became scared and very unsociable. I had one good friend who knew that I had changed, but I couldn't tell her why; I didn't want my brother to die. It changed me so much. All through my teenage years I was terrified of boys, and if they tried to touch me or suggested any form of physical relationship, I was off!

At 18 I met my husband-to-be. We had sex after three months. It wasn't as bad as I thought it would be, but I still cried afterwards alone in the bathroom. I still kept the pain hidden deep within me for fear of my brother being killed in an accident. I was always watching to make sure he was safe – and when he joined the Army I was terrified because his friend, 'the rapist', joined up at the same time.

I am happily married now. I have four children who are all doing well and hopefully have not been damaged by the sometimes 'weird' behaviour of their mother.

At 32, after the birth of my fourth child, I just couldn't cope. I became so depressed, and my doctor put in down to postnatal depression, but I knew deep down that it was more than that, so I decided to look into some form of counselling or talking therapy. I was lucky enough to find a counsellor who specialised in issues like rape and historic abuse.

I remember the first session. It was extremely scary and I cried a lot. The counsellor sat and listened and didn't say much at all. She didn't finish my sentences off for me or give me any advice. She just sat and she listened. No one as far as I could remember had ever done that. Consequent sessions were slightly easier, as I trawled though my past, raking stuff up that stung and stabbed in places within me that I had thought were untouchable. Because of the passage of time, it was hard to even say the word 'rape', but I will never forget how I felt walking out of that place after about the fifth session, disclosing the events of the rape 18 years before. It felt like a weight had lifted. I had dumped it onto someone else to carry, and it was brilliant.

I almost bounced home. Once the counselling had ended, I started to open up to my husband and even found the courage to tell my brother. He cried at what I had kept hidden for so long in order to 'save his life'. None of us have ever seen 'the rapist' and don't even know if he is still alive. I am very much alive, and so is my brother.

Marianne

I went for professional counselling because I knew that there was something troubling me that I had not talked about. I felt ashamed and needed to 'spill the beans', so to speak. Many years before I had lived at a friend's house. I was about 24 and had lodged at her house for about a year. We worked together running a small café, and we were great friends. My friend had recently taken up with a new boyfriend, a builder on the site where our business was, who had decided to move in. He was okay and built like a shed. He could be very temperamental, but he was charming and had a great sense of humour. At the weekends we would all go out to a local workingmen's club, meet other friends, dance and enjoy a few drinks. I was young and naïve and cherished the freedom that living at my friend's house gave me.

One Monday morning, I woke up with the most horrendous hangover. In fact I now recall it as my first and last. I came downstairs and my friend took one look at me and said: 'Oh Marianne you can't possibly come to work like that. You look green,' (at which point I went and threw up outside in the garden). 'Go back to bed. It shouldn't be too busy today.'

That was all I needed to hear. I was off back up those stairs feeling like absolute death. I must have fallen into a deep sleep, because before I knew it, it was 11am. I went downstairs, thankful that at least my head had started to clear. Every fibre in me was screaming out for coffee. Putting the kettle on, I washed a mug and at that moment I had a sense that I was being watched. As I turned round, there was Doug, my friend's new man, a thick-set giant, standing with his arm against the doorframe, completely taking up the whole space. Thoughts quickly raced through my mind. I was panicking and instinctively frightened: what was he doing here? Why wasn't he at work? I wanted to get out of there as fast as I could, but there was nowhere to run, nowhere to hide, I was standing in a baggy t-shirt, and he stood there watching me. Nervously I asked: 'Can I get you a cup of tea, Doug?'

There was no answer and no time to get away. Three times over a two-hour period, he lunged at me and grabbed me, throwing me onto the hard floor, right there, in the kitchen. After he raped me, over and over again, he carried me upstairs to the bathroom, where I vividly remember him locking the door. He placed the toilet lid down and told me to sit there and wait. I was too frightened to do anything else.

And then he calmly ran a bath; he put bubble bath in it and even tested the temperature. I was so confused by this man. On reflection I must have been in shock. And then in a surreal moment he picked me up and gently lowered me into the bath, gently washing me. I was terrified. The inconsistency of this man was so confusing.

While he was doing this 'washing' thing, he started to tell me how he loved my friend and how sad and how angry she would be if she ever found out that I had come on to him in such a sly way behind her back. I was convinced that it was my fault, absolutely convinced, so I never told a soul until I went to see a counsellor. The counsellor asked me what my story was and what had brought me to counselling.

I told the story as above and explained that I had been having nightmares recently and in fact had been having them since the incident 24 years previously. I had a real aversion to having a bath, and if I did ever manage it, I couldn't stand for the toilet lid to be down or for the bathroom door to be locked.

The counsellor was a nice man who listened intently. When I had finished talking, he said, 'Would you like to try a technique that may lessen the impact of all those memories?' I said I would try anything, so he relaxed me to a deep level and then he asked me to relive the incident on an imaginary screen and afterwards to rewind it. I did this technique a couple of times and then booked another appointment. Two days later I felt the best I had ever felt and rang to cancel my next appointment. He was happy for me to do so and said he had expected it. It was brilliant. I have never looked back. I could still recall the incident and describe the details, but it has no emotional impact on me any more.

Kelly

She had a sense of being on water, floating, bobbing, eyelids shut tight, laying, unable to move, floating in darkness. Pain, so much pain, drifting in and out of consciousness, trying to remember, too much effort. She said she couldn't think straight. She couldn't think at all. She had no memory, just unrelenting pain... She recalled glimpses of terror from somewhere, then vagueness and empty darkness all around her.

Kelly had woken up or shall we say, become conscious, at exactly 4 o'clock on a Sunday morning. Later she had been able to recall these details because she had heard a radio quite nearby to wherever she was. It was only fleeting, maybe a car had pulled up and gone again, but she definitely heard the pips of a news announcement.

Lifting her head slowly, she still couldn't see much. Her eyes seemed to be stuck together apart from a thin sliver of light, which penetrated through the gap into her eyeball like a knife. She could smell the sea, and the metallic taste in her mouth made her feel instantly sick. Vomiting in the space where she lay, the spasms in her stomach prompted Kelly to try to move, and she managed to get to her knees. It was agony but she did it.

She soon began to realise that she *was* actually on a vessel of sorts on the water and the tiny amount of light and vague outlines of buildings that she could see made her think that she was on some sort of boat. With her hands she precariously felt the surface around her which was cold, hard, damp metal. She could hear 'click, click, click' sounds in the gentle wind, which with her knowledge of boats she thought must be halyards and the familiar sound of high-pitched gulls crying from above. All of this kept her mind active as she lay wondering if this was the place where she would die.

'You alright, love?' came a voice from above her.

'Help me, please help me!' she screamed, as her physical body reacted, shaking profusely.

Within what seemed like hours, but in reality was only 17 minutes, Kelly heard more than one siren and what sounded like the blades of a helicopter in the sky. From the many television rescue programmes she'd watched in her 27 years, she knew this was a rescue. She would be safe and with this knowledge, she passed out.

Four days later, Kelly awoke in a room surrounded by her family, her fiancé Lucas and three police officers. As she opened her eyes, the light stung, but she needed to know her mum was really there, feeling the sting of her tears as they rolled down her bruised and battered skin. She knew she was alive and could see the beautiful albeit worried faces of her family.

It took more than three weeks before the police were able to take an overview and concise statement, because Kelly's recollection of events took a while to come, thanks to the knowledge in the field of trauma and complete dedication of the female lead investigation officer, who knew that victims aren't always able to recall details immediately and may or may not return.

Kelly had been out all day with her friends on the Saturday of the incident. They'd been shopping in their seaside hometown. Later they went for afternoon tea and scones in the coffee lounge of a place called the Flitz Hotel. They had decided to go for a drink later to 'The Scarlet', so they went home to Molly's flat in the middle of town to leave their shopping and get changed.

It had been a long time since Kelly had been out with her girlfriends, as she and Lucas were planning to marry, and all of their time over the past six months had been taken up with wedding preparations.

The Scarlet was a new venue in town, open since the previous New Year. It was a pub-cum-nightclub with three different levels, offering food, drinks and cocktails as well as a choice of dance or more quiet settings away from bright flashing lights and chaos. Kelly recalled being in a section called the snug. Over a drink, she was catching up with her two friends, Molly and Jess, reminiscing about their school days and the antics they got up to. Three young men and a woman came over and gestured to sit and talk with them. They were friendly enough, and Kelly related that she got on well with the woman who she thought was called Megan, although her memory of this was hazy.

Molly, a single mum, had received a WhatsApp message and picture of a tantrum-stamping child from her Dad saying that she needed to come home as her son Reece was playing up, and he couldn't cope any more. Jess went with Molly, and Kelly decided to stay out with her new friend Megan. The five who were left carried on drinking into the night.

Kelly's memory of what happened next was distorted. She remembered wanting to go home and looking for her phone to call a taxi. Megan, or whatever her name was, had said she would get her home safely. As she gave her verbal statement and with her eyes closed she could picture herself falling, not being able to stand or walk properly. She had a vague recollection of two of the men helping her into what she thought was a taxi.

But then the woman, Megan, was driving and she had intermittent glimpses of being sexually assaulted by the woman and then one or two of the men. They were brutal, especially the woman. From her vague memory, she recalled that they weren't in the car any more. They were in a kind of storage unit, and the largest of the men was raping her, slapping and punching her in her face as he did. She remembered the pain across her eyes, and they were still painful as tears continued to flow. He was telling her that she needed to learn a lesson or two, and she could hear the woman in the background saying: 'Give it to her. Who does she think she is? We'll see that she doesn't make it to no poncy wedding.'

Kelly's next recollection caused her to sit bolt upright in bed during the interview as she remembered being picked up by each of her hands and feet and thrown over the side of the quay.

The thought that these strangers had not only raped and beaten her to within an inch of her life, but the fact that they were intent on leaving her to drown, was too much to take in. Kelly became distraught, and the nurse asked for the police to stop the interview, but she insisted on carrying on as she wanted to get it over with.

Someone must have been looking out for her that night, because she didn't end up in the sea, but in the bottom of a fishing boat called 'Geordie's Catch'. The tide had been out, so landing on the hard steel boat 15 feet down added to her already life-changing injuries.

Kelly had sustained a broken pelvis and hip, she had four broken ribs, her arm was fractured in two places and both knees and ankles were broken. She lost three fingers and sustained a fractured skull. She had been so brutally raped that she had severe permanent internal injuries to both her anal and vaginal areas. Her head and face were so swollen that she was only able to eat through a tube.

It was eighteen months later that Kelly sat across from me in the therapy room. As she related her experience, it was clear that although physically she had recovered quite well, psychologically she had not even started. Her symptoms included:

- Sleep disturbance: no REM sleep and inability to process the traumatic information

- Panic attacks: reliving the incident

- Rumination: thinking about the attack and what she did to deserve it

- Hypervigilance: constant state of alertness

- Triggered responses: sound of gulls, radio playing and boats on the television

- Fear of going out: terror of it happening again/repercussions

- Fear of being alone: terror of it happening again/repercussions

- Anxiety: over-firing of the flight or fight response

• Depression: lack of focus on her future.

We worked with Jigsaw's Three Point Turnaround System©
(see Appendix 10). The intervention we used was a series of EMDR
over 15 sessions and a complete one-hour long session of the
repeated Visual Kinesthetic Dissociation (VKD) technique.

This is Kelly's completed evaluation of her experience, using
the Three Point Turnaround System©.

Initial Assessment and Sexual Assault Trauma Line
1 – 100% - *99%*

Ability to work productively and progressively
1 – 100% - *99%*

How much progress have you made towards recovery?
1 – 100% - *100%*

Please answer the following open questions to the best of your
ability by being as open and as honest as possible.

What part of the work you have undertaken has helped you the
most and why?
*I found the whole experience of EMDR both frightening and
releasing, because I had to relive every second of the attack. It
brought up stuff that I hadn't remembered previously, and this
was a huge shock. It was the beginning of recovery for me, hard
though it was at the time.*

What part of the work, if any, did you find was not useful and why?

Even though the EMDR was good in dealing with what happened to me, what really helped my sloop and panic attacks was the time after we did that rewind thing. It seemed to take the violence and horror out of it. I can still talk about it now but I don't get upset. It's like telling someone else's story.

Do you feel able to move on to a new part in your life, leaving the traumatic incidents of the past behind you?

Yes definitely, I am able to go out now, in the last few weeks I have been going out on my own.

Is there anything else or other therapy that you feel you might need to additionally assist with your recovery and restoration into a new and fulfilling life?

No, I'm ready to move on with my life now.

Is there anything else that you would like to add regarding the treatment and/or processing interventions that you have been given?

I feel like I was treated really well and my only disappointment was that I wasn't offered any psychological help earlier on.

12

Working with Those Affected by Sexual Violence

There is no one way to work with a person who has been the target of the trauma of rape and/or sexual violence. Most important is that clients are treated with respect and not rushed into disclosing information they may have kept deeply buried for many years. To suddenly feel under pressure to have to recall their experience can often be unhelpful at the beginning of engaging in therapy or support work in any field of care.

Recognition that each victim is unique and will respond differently is key in the initial stages of assistance. It is useful to have a metaphorical bag of 'processing tools' allowing the professional to identify which intervention will suit which individual.

For many years now, collectively, the professional staff that represent a diverse set of backgrounds and experience at Jigsaw have personally worked with several hundred victims of rape and/or s exual violence. Our metaphorical tool bags have started with general, post-trauma counselling skills, guided visualisation and relaxation techniques.

In the early days we realised that there had to be a more effective way to work with the consequences of rape and sexual violence that would allow individuals to reclaim the power taken away from them and to rebuild their lives in the best way for them.

The following are vital dos and don'ts for working with those affected by rape and/or sexual violence:

1. Do listen effectively, so that if you had to recall the client's story you would be able to do so without leaving anything out.

2. Do acknowledge, understand and believe the client's recollection of their experience, even if it sounds completely outside of what you would consider to be 'normal'.

3. Do work through the client's expectations of the work you are about to do, so that you both know which aims you are working towards.

4. Do allow the client to work at a pace and time to suit them, expalining what is and what is not possible within that time limit.

5. Do implement safe boundaries at the beginning of any work, so as to keep the client safe from further harm. These are limits that ensure you are working safely and ethically.

6. Don't make promises that you are unable to keep. The client may have already been let down many times, and this will further embed trust issues for them.

7. Don't attempt to work with any issues around rape and/or sexual violence that you have not received the training for, as this may hinder the client's fragile healing process.

8. Don't bring your own personal issues or experiences into any work that you are doing with a person who has been the target of rape or sexual violation.

9. Don't judge, advise or tell a target of rape and/or sexual assault what they should do. If you are unable to assist this person, then signpost to suitable organisations such as a rape crisis centre or sexual health clinic. Allow them to make their own choices to suit their own needs.

10. Don't work without clinical supervision, peer support or case management.

A basic knowledge and understanding of all of the techniques and interventions listed in this book is highly recommended in order to be able to assist those affected by sexual assault. Remember that you may be held accountable if the treatment you provide causes further disturbance.

When a survivor of childhood rape and sexual assault develops into adulthood, they learn to cope in many different ways. Some bury the traumatic experiences deep within them. Some say that they are able to forget that the assaults ever happened, which is often highly dependent on their circumstances and their network of support. Most, however, are unable to cope with 'normal life' and constantly suffer as a result.

Working in this field of trauma, you may witness in the client's voice or in the way that they present physically, an essence of the unfulfilled childhood. The way that they act or respond to any therapy or work that they are doing with you may certainly present as that of the child they were at the time of the sexually abusive assaults rather than as the adult in front of you.

By working with such a survivor using an inner-child script, he/she is able to relax into a safe inner world, to a place and time in their formative years, where the assaults may have been perpetrated upon them regularly.

Facilitating the adult in front of you to meet with their inner child at a specific time within those abusive childhood years and encouraging them to come face to face, for the adult to nurture the 'lost' child, engaging, holding and merging them together as one, has the ability to fast-track their recovery and open up an awakening within them.

Treatment matching

No one size of treatment will ever fit all and in some cases none of the treatments featured in this publication will work at all for some people.

My general rule-of-thumb list of intervention for treating rape and sexual violence-related trauma is not exhaustive, as new styles are developed and we gain new metaphoric tools after each continuing professional development session we attend.

Whatever intervention is provided to assist a victim of rape and/or sexual violence, it has to be right for them, providing choice, enablying them to work with their own post traumatic growth at an individual suitable pace, in order to make a choice to rebuild their lives and move on to live the fulfilling and complete life they deserve.

Training for all of the interventions covered in this book is easily accessible and I have listed a few of the trainers available at the time of writing. However, trainers and organisations change constantly, so it is also worth doing some internet research for yourself before committing to any training.

Although new treatments and interventions are being researched all the time, there are already many interventions that have been shown to be effective for working with those affected by rape and/or sexual violence. These include the following:

Critical incident debriefing (CID) or psychological debriefing

This is for use with groups, especially in the aftermath of workplace fatalities and critical incidents, disasters, fire or suicide of an employee. The idea with group intervention is to go into a workplace setting and assist, putting in place a structured diffusion initially to take the heat out of the situation. During this time the debriefer can assess those who stand out in the groups as possibly needing individual assistance.

Eye movement desensitisation reprocessing (EMDR)

This is an excellent intervention for multiple traumas to suit individuals who were sexually abused over a period of time in their childhood, those who have experienced bullying, survivors of domestic violence, CCTV operators who regularly witness life-threatening events, military personnel, emergency services personnel, traffic police, disaster response teams and therapists.[1]

---

1   For further information and training, see www.emdr-training.com

Brain spotting (BSP)

This is a relatively new intervention which works on the basis of releasing the body from the traumatic memories it holds via the neurobiological pathway. I find it to be a useful tool for working with adult survivors of sexual assault, because the client doesn't necessarily need to speak. Their body tells the story and in doing so they are able to release many years of pent-up stagnant and toxic agony.[2]

Visual kinaesthetic (VK) dissociation technique

This is a specific intervention for single traumas such as rape, kidnap, torture, sexual violence, road traffic collision, personal assault or injury, sudden death, shock of suicide or other shocks to the system.[3]

Relaxation and/or mindfulness

I use both of these all the time for treating trauma and usually at the first couple of sessions to teach the client how to ground themselves and be relaxed. Only by remaining calm can we even begin to assist the chaos of a person's damaged psyche. I would use these alongside other treatments, for example the rewind technique works twice as well if combined with a deep relaxation process as does CID with individuals.[4]

Sensorimotor psychotherapy

Sensorimotor psychotherapy is a therapy developed by Dr Pat Ogden that works somatically (physiological memory) with both the mind and body, so that the traumatic memory can be processed effectively, allowing for lessened impact, thus leaving no residue of the traumatic memory.[5]

---

2   For further information and training, see www.brainspotting.pro or www.brainspotting.co.uk

3   For further information and training, see www.davidmuss.co.uk

4   For further information and training, see www.mindfulnessassociation.net

5   For further information and training, see www.sensorimotorpsychotherapy.org

Guided visualisation

This is very powerful tool to assist clients, especially when dealing with childhood trauma such as sexual assault. It allows the client to go back, to revisit and to make changes in situations that they were not able to do anything about as children. It's useful to have some music in the background, and I always have soft blankets available, as many people feel quite exposed when they have their eyes closed.[6]

Post-trauma counselling

I would use this as a skills-based intervention with every client at some level, though almost never on its own, as for some clients with deeply embedded trauma just talking and going over feelings can cause an abreaction, which can be detrimental for the client, who then goes home and has to deal with it on their own.

---

6   For further information and training, see www.holistic-community.co.uk

Conclusion

When someone tells you that they have been raped or sexually violated, whether as an adult or a child, it can be like being passed a box containing a fragile glass ball. They are telling you about their experience because they trust you to hold the fragility of that glass ball with every ounce of care, understanding and kindness that you can muster. Whatever you do, be careful not to break that glass, shattering what self-worth and courage the client has bravely managed to hang on to until this point.

The honest and very real expectation of each and every survivor is quite simply that they will be treated with respect, dignity and basic human kindness. If, for whatever reason, you are not able to provide this then you can refer on just as kindly.

Personally I've been working with the courage and bravery of those affected by rape and sexual violence since 1996. In that time I have witnessed such countless unfathomable depths of sadness, pain and despair that I have been on the verge of giving up many times. But always during this pattern of thought, well-meaning colleagues and/or valuable time in clinical supervision have offered a fragment of encouragement to keep working. However, the genuine inspiration would come from a random card, letter or a simple email from someone who had passed through our doors along their healing and recovery journey, saying how much they had gained from the work, or repeating a nugget of wisdom that may have helped them somehow during a particular dark time in their life.

It's fair to say that professionals working in this field need to have a prerequisite to believe everything that they are told, to let go of judgements and to be in awe of the survivors of rape and sexual violence who sit or stand before them, because these are the real warriors, the strong and the courageous. They have been through the most horrifying ordeals – the most invasive and physically abusive assaults – and they have survived. We are but a conduit of their onward journey to recovery. Give courage, respect and understanding always to these heroic individuals.

And so, if I were asked to relay one message as a voice from all of those who have been targeted by sexual violation in any way, it would be that kindness, encouragement and to be believed is critical for all recovery.

Appendix 1

Sexual Abuse Timeline

Article II.

Birth
|
Childhood
|
Adolescence/ School/ Care Home
|
College/ University/ Prison
|
Significant Relationships
|
Deaths/ Bereavements
|
Trauma/s

Suggest that the client relates all of their traumas throughout their lifetime, and work with processing the worst trauma first.

Appendix 2

Impact of Event Scale (IES)

Throughout life, people experience very difficult times and when those difficulties are borne of an act of invasive, sexually violent, physical trauma, it can result in devastating psychological issues that interrupt their day to day function. With the right assistance though, these issues can and are resolved with effective and well researched interventions that facilitate the processing of traumatic information, allowing the client time and space to work towards trauma focused recovery and restoration.

For professionals working in this field, having a measuring tool to assess the impact and identification of an individual's emotional response to a sexually violent traumatic incident can be extremely useful. However, it is of equal importance to be aware that each person is unique in how they respond and that any measuring tool must be used as a 'guide only' to assist in history and information taking and not as a diagnostic tool for labelling a client with a 'disorder'.

Below is a link to numerous measuring tools of which, many would be of use in the field of rape, sexual violence and survivors of childhood sexual assault and abuse.

To find a List of all measures - PTSD: National Center for PTSD http://www.ptsd.va.gov/professional/assessment/documents/DRRI2scales.pdf

Reference

Vogt, D., Smith, B. N., King, D. W., & King, L. A. (2012). The Deployment Risk and Resilience Inventory-2 (DRRI-2) [Measurement instrument]. Available from http://www.ptsd.va.gov, accessed on 20 October 2016.

Appendix 3

Trauma Tapestry©: A Seven-Step Process

1. Establish if the client enjoys or is good at drawing and explain how the Trauma Tapestry works from beginning to end and that this is not a quick fix; there is no time limit. This intervention works really well with those who have been affected by childhood sexual abuse.

2. Suggest to the client that he/she starts to draw images of the rape, sexual violence or abuse from childhood and to bring to subsequent sessions.

3. Together in the sessions start to join the pictures together with tape in exactly the order that the client wants.

4. If the client is happy to continue with the drawings and to bring them in to each session to go through you can explore their reasons for choosing certain colours.

5. Ask the client if it is okay for you to keep the tapestry in the safekeeping of your premises, so that they are not constantly looking at the pictures they have already drawn. Guard it with your life. How you take care of the client's work is reflective of how you might be seen to take care of the client.

6. Give or agree to post the completed tapestry to the client by Recorded Mail, so that they can find a safe place to set light to it. Suggestions might be to carry this out in a metal bin or incinerator. It is crucial that the ashes are saved.

7. Keep in mind that the client must then decide what to do with the ashes and why, for example:

- Put the ashes into a pot or into the earth and grow a plant so that something beautiful comes from something not so beautiful.

- Put the ashes into a piece of muslin and tie to an air balloon and let it go, watching until it disappears out of sight.

- Take the ashes in a box or an envelope to a significant place or the where the attack/s happened and leave or scatter them there.

- Put the ashes in the toilet, skip, rubbish dump – anywhere that is significant.

- Release the ashes into a river or stream (making sure there is no plastic contained within it).

Appendix 4

Writing a Symbolic Letter

Ask the client if they would like to write a symbolic letter to the sexual perpetrator/s (never to be sent) starting with their name or the name that the client chooses to call them, for example slug, roach, amoeba, maggot.

Example symbolic letter:

Hi Maggot Skin,

This letter has been a long time coming, even now when I think of what you did to me it makes my skin crawl. How dare you think that you would have ever got away with doing such vile things to a small child in your supposed care? You sicko...!

Well now I look at you through the eyes of an adult, and I see you for what you are, a sick individual who was so sexually inadequate and unable to get a girlfriend, so you obviously turned your attention to children. How many is it now that you have abused? Oh yes, 24 at the last count, and they kept letting you out to do it again and again. Well, not this time, you piece of shit. Nineteen years in a hell hole where you will be buggered and violated just like I was by you.

They say that to get the best revenge is to live well, and believe me, I am. I've had the best help, so that I no longer stay awake every night recalling the despicable things that you did to me in my little pink nightdress. I only hope I never have to see you in person because I can't say what I would do. Probably laugh in your pathetic face and walk away because you are not worth anything more than that.

I can live my life now as free as a bird, full of fun and laughter with my family and friends who also think you are a pathetic waste of space.

With all the best from your once Child Victim,

Casey

Only if the client is happy to do so, suggest that he/she brings the letter in so that you can read it back to him/her. Discuss their thoughts and feelings upon doing this. Then ask them to take it away and burn it and retain the ashes and then encourage them to make a decision as to what they would like to do with those ashes in order for them to feel that they have released the energy invested in the symbolic letter.

Before you see them, again ask that they carry out their wishes as to what to do with the ashes.

Appendix 5

Generic Guided Visualisation for Adult Survivors of Childhood Sexual Violation

OKAY, SO JUST RELAX NOW. TAKE A DEEP BREATHE IN THROUGH YOUR NOSE DOWN INTO YOUR STOMACH FOR THE COUNT OF SEVEN AND THEN GENTLY RELEASE THAT BREATH OUT THROUGH YOUR MOUTH FOR THE COUNT OF ELEVEN. REPEAT THIS AGAIN UNTIL YOU FEEL NICELY RELAXED.

NOW VISUALISATION IS NOT THE SAME AS BEING ASLEEP. IT'S LIKE A DREAM – ALL YOU NEED TO DO IS JUST LET THE RELAXATION TAKE OVER AND SEE WHAT COMES UP FOR YOU IN YOUR MIND'S EYE, IT'S A BIT LIKE HAVING A STORY READ OUT LOUD TO YOU.

YOU WILL STILL BE AWARE, AND YOU WILL BE ABLE TO HEAR EVERYTHING I SAY TO YOU… CHANGES WITHIN YOU MAY BE DREAMY AND FLOATY. ALL YOU NEED TO DO IS JUST RELAX, RELAX AND RELAX.

AS YOUR SUBCONSCIOUS MIND TAKES IN AND HEARS EVERYTHING, YOUR CONSCIOUS MIND MAY JUST DRIFT OFF INTO A WORLD OF ITS OWN. SO AS YOU CONTINUE TO MAKE YOURSELF AS COMFORTABLE AS POSSIBLE…

(MUSIC)

SO CARRY ON AND MAKE YOURSELF COMFORTABLE, WITH YOUR EYES CLOSED, PAY ATTENTION TO YOUR BREATHING. YOU CAN JUST LET GO, LET GO AND

RELAX RELAX... THE MORE YOU RELAX THE BETTER YOU WILL FEEL AND THE BETTER YOU FEEL THE MORE YOU WILL RELAX.

WHEN WE HAVE FINISHED, YOU WILL WAKE UP REFRESHED AND CALM WITH A SENSE OF INNER PEACE. SO NOW, NOTICE YOUR BREATHING (SPEECH SLOWING) – THE GENTLE UP AND DOWN OF YOUR CHEST AS YOUR BREATHING HAPPENS ALL BY ITSELF. (SPEECH SLOWING)

JUST FOLLOW MY VOICE AS I COUNT BACKWARDS FROM FIFTEEN, AND BY THE TIME WE REACH ONE YOU WILL BE RELAXING DEEPER AND DEEPER THAN YOU EVER HAVE BEFORE. AND I WILL BEGIN THAT COUNT NOW 15, 14, 13, 12, GENTLY RELAXING NOW, 11, DOWN AND DOWN, 10, THAT'S RIGHT, 9, COUNTING BACKWARDS, 8, ONLY AS FAST AS, 7, YOU BEGIN TO... DEEPLY RELAX ALL OF YOUR FACIAL MUSCLES...THOSE SMALLER MUSCLES DOWN THROUGH THE RELAXATION IN YOUR NECK (VOICE SLOWING) INTO YOUR SHOULDERS, YOUR TORSO, RELAXATION SPREADING THROUGHOUT YOUR ARMS AND DOWN, DOWN, DOWN INTO YOUR HANDS AND FINGERS, RELAXING YOU MORE AND MORE INTO A WONDERFUL DAYDREAM, A STORY, YOUR STORY.

JUST LET GO –AND ALLOW THE GENTLE LIGHTNESS OF LETTING GO OF ALL NEGATIVE THOUGHTS FEELINGS AS YOU DESCEND INTO HAPPINESS, SAFETY AND LOVE...

LET THAT RELAXATION MOVE DOWN INTO YOUR LEGS, RIGHT DOWN NOW, THROUGH INTO YOUR CALVES YOUR ANKLES AND INTO THE TINY MUSCLES AND BONES OF YOUR FEET AND DOWN TO THE VERY ENDS OF YOUR TOES.

WITHOUT THINKING, RELAX, RELAX AND RELAX, FLOATING, SOFTNESS AND GENTLENESS RELAX RELAX...TOWARDS YOUR OWN SAFETY, SOFTNESS AND RECOVERY...ALLOW THE RELAXATION TO SPREAD

THROUGHOUT YOUR BODY INTO EVERY CELL, EVERY MUSCLE AND BONE...THROUGHOUT YOUR SKIN AND YOUR COMPLETE BODY...

AS YOU ARE RELAXED THERE, AND I AM TALKING HERE...KEEP NOTICING YOUR BREATHING... NOTICE HOW YOU FEEL YOURSELF SINKING DEEPER DOWN WITH EVERY OUT BREATH...THAT'S RIGHT, WELL DONE, YOU'RE DOING FINE...

NOW I WANT YOU TO MAKE YOUR BODY AS COMFORTABLE AS POSSIBLE...FROM THE TOP OF YOUR HEAD IMAGINE A SPECIAL RELAXING AND WARMING BEAM OF LIGHT IS SHINING DOWN ON YOU...IT'S GOING TO MOVE DOWN YOUR BODY SLOWLY AND AS IT SHINES DOWN ON YOU YOUR BODY CAN WARM AND RELAX.... BIT BY BIT...IMAGINE THE WARMTH OF THE LIGHT SHINING ON YOUR HEAD AND FACE...THE COLOUR AS IT GENTLY RELAXES YOU EVEN MORE...NOW LET THAT LIGHT FLOW DOWN AND DOWN THROUGH YOUR BODY AND YOU CAN CONTINUE TO FEEL THE WARMTH AS IT GOES DOWN THROUGH YOUR NECK AND SHOULDERS... AND DOWN IN TO YOUR CHEST...RELAXING THE MUSCLES OF YOUR STOMACH AND YOUR BREATHING GOES ON ALL BY ITSELF...DOWN INTO YOUR ARMS... YOUR HANDS AND THE TIPS OF YOUR FINGERS AS IT RELAXES EACH MUSCLE EACH FIBRE...DOWN THROUGH YOUR LEGS AND KNEES AND CALVES AND RIGHT DOWN INTO YOUR FEET AND TOES RELAXING YOU MORE AND MORE...THAT'S GREAT NOW...AND NOW YOUR BODY IS NICE AND RELAXED...YOU CAN TAKE YOURSELF SOMEWHERE UP INTO YOUR MIND AND IMAGINE THAT YOU ARE OUTSIDE SOMEWHERE IN A GARDEN ON A WARM SUNNY DAY. THIS MAY BE A SPECIAL PLACE FOR YOU OR SOMEWHERE IN YOUR IMAGINATION.

IMAGINE A GENTLE BREEZE BLOWING AS YOU SIT OUTSIDE SOMEWHERE BEAUTIFUL, FEEL IT AS IT

BLOWS THROUGH YOUR HAIR, ACROSS YOUR FACE...OK NOW I WANT YOU TO IMAGINE THAT YOU ARE LOOKING UP INTO THE SKY...

REMEMBERING HAPPY TIMES IN THE PAST WHEN YOU WERE RELAXED...NOTHING AT ALL TO DO... NOTHING AT ALL TO WORRY ABOUT...FEELING REALLY GOOD ABOUT YOURSELF...AND WHILE YOU ARE HERE WITH ME RELAXED, SAFE AND PROTECTED, RELAXED AND AT EASE JUST LET YOUR MIND DRIFT BACK IN TIME...BACK IN TIME AS THOUGH THERE WERE NO SUCH THING AS TIME...BACK INTO THE YEARS THAT HAVE GONE... ALL THE WAY BACK TO YOUR OWN FORMING... DEVELOPING...IMPRESSIONABLE YEARS OF YOUTH...HOW QUICK TO AROUSE...HOW SUDDEN TO CHANGE...REMEMBER HOW WHEN YOU WERE VERY YOUNG...HOW YOU COULD CHANGE FROM LOVING ONE MOMENT TO HATING THE NEXT...REMEMBER WHEN EVERYTHING WAS SO VERY NEW...WHEN IT WAS ALL FOR THE FIRST TIME...THE FIRST DAY AT YOUR FIRST SCHOOL...THE STRANGENESS AND NEWNESS OF IT ALL...REMEMBER AGAIN CHANGING SCHOOLS TO THE BIG SCHOOL...AGAIN SO STRANGE AND NEW... AND REMEMBER LEAVING SCHOOL AND STARTING WORK...JUST AS STRANGE...JUST AS NEW...AND ALL THE FIRST TIMES AND NEW EXPERIENCES...LET YOUR MIND GO TO AN AGE THAT YOU CAN MOST REMEMBER AND WHEN YOU ARRIVE AT THAT AGE, TELL ME, TELL ME ABOUT A PLACE WHERE YOU WOULD GO ON YOUR OWN WHEN YOU WERE SAD, SCARED OR UNHAPPY...

The client may answer with one with one of many places, however it is most often a memory of their bedroom or place of safety (bear in mind that sexual assaults often happen in children's bedrooms). Follow the steps as below and get them to build a clear picture in their mind.

- BEDROOM? STAIRS?

- ALLOW THE CLIENT TO BUILD A CLEAR PICTURE OF THAT PLACE: TELL ME...WHAT WAS THAT PLACE LIKE?

- WHAT WAS THE WALLPAPER LIKE?

- WHAT COLOUR WAS IT?

- FURNITURE?

- CARPET?

- WINDOW?

- WHAT COULD YOU SEE FROM THE WINDOW?

- YOUR POSITION? AND TELL ME NOW, AS YOU SEE YOURSELF AS THAT LITTLE GIRL/BOY, WHAT ARE YOU WEARING? COLOUR?

OKAY, AND NOW JUST SEE YOURSELF SITTING IN THIS PLACE THINKING ABOUT ALL THE THINGS THAT HAPPENED OR WERE HAPPENING AT THAT TIME, FEELING ALL THOSE FEELINGS JUST AS YOU DID THEN. CAN YOU SEE THAT? SO NOW I WANT YOU TO GO THERE TO THAT PLACE, TO THE SMALLER YOU AS THE ADULT YOU ARE TODAY AND I WANT YOU TO WALK OVER TO THE LITTLE CHILD YOU WERE THEN AND SIT DOWN AT THE SIDE OF HIM/HER, PUT YOUR ARM AROUND HIM/HER, HOLD HIM/HER TIGHT, AND TELL HIM/HER EVERYTHING HE/SHE WANTED TO KNOW AND FEEL FREE TO DO THAT ALOUD OR IN YOUR OWN HEAD AND BE SURE TO TELL HIM/HER THAT EVERYTHING IS GOING TO BE ALRIGHT...AND YOU KNOW MORE THAN I DO EXACTLY WHAT HE/SHE WANTED AND NEEDED TO HEAR THEN, SO TELL HIM/HER......AND KEEP HOLDING HIM/HER IN YOUR ARMS AS YOU DO, LOVING HIM/HER, EVEN HOLDING ON TO HIM/HER SO TIGHT THAT YOU CAN IMAGINE PULLING HIM/HER BACK INSIDE WHERE HE/SHE BELONGS AND YOU CAN TAKE HIM/HER DOWN TO A WARM SAFE PLACE DEEP INSIDE YOU WHERE

HE/SHE WILL BE SAFE AND PROTECTED AND ALLOW HIM/HER NOW TO SLEEP PEACEFULLY WITHIN YOU BECAUSE HE/SHE'S BEEN OUTSIDE FOR A LONG TIME AND IT'S NOW TIME FOR YOU TO TAKE CARE OF HIM/HER AND ALLOW THE REAL YOU TO EVOLVE IN THE WAY HE/SHE WANTS TO...BECAUSE I KNOW THAT YOU WANT TO TAKE GOOD CARE OF HIM/HER, AND FROM THIS DAY FORWARD YOU CAN JUST LET GO AND NOT ALLOW ANYONE OR ANYTHING TO HOLD YOU BACK FROM HAVING A FULL AND HAPPY LIFE...IT'S YOUR TURN NOW TO BE HAPPY WITH YOUR LIFE IN THE WAY YOU CHOOSE TO LIVE IT FOR YOURSELF AND TO ENJOY EVERY MOMENT...BECAUSE YOU KNOW...YOUR LIFE CAN BE WHATEVER YOU WANT IT TO BE AND THESE NEW FEELINGS OF INNER HAPPINESS AND COMPLETE FREEDOM AND OF KNOWING THAT YOUR NEW FUTURE IS FULL OF LOVE AND FRESH OPPORTUNITIES...SAFETY WILL BE ALL AROUND YOU AS YOU WILL FEEL A NEW SENSE OF POSITIVITY IN YOUR LIFE AS YOU GO DEEPER AND DEEPER...STAYING IN A PLACE OF TRANQUILITY AND RELEASE AND DEEP RELAXATION...AND NOW I AM GOING TO BE QUIET FOR A FEW MOMENTS WHILE YOU TAKE TIME TO MAKE PEACE WITH YOURSELF AND YOUR INNER CHILD AND JUST USE THIS TIME FOR YOU TO TAKE YOUR TIME...SO JUST RELAX NOW UNTIL YOU HEAR MY VOICE AGAIN...IT WILL SOON BE TIME FOR YOU TO AWAKEN...I WILL AWAKEN YOU BY COUNTING YOU UP A SET OF NUBERS   FROM ONE TO TEN...USING EACH STEP AS A NUMBER...YOU WILL FEEL AND BECOME...MORE AND MORE AWAKE AND ALERT...YOU WILL BE IN FULL CONTROL OF YOUR BODY...AND OF YOUR MIND...FEELING...REFRESHED...CONFIDENT...AND YET FILLED WITH ENERGY...ONE...TWO...GRADUALLY...AWAKENING...THREE...FEELING...WONDERFUL...FOUR...FIVE...SIX...MORE AND MORE AWAKE REFRESHED AND ALERT...SEVEN...

FEELING GREAT...EIGHT NEARLY AWAKE NOW...NINE... OPENING YOUR EYES NOW AND...TEN...RETURNING TO NORMAL WAKEFUL AWARENESS...

Appendix 6

Specific Guided Visualisation for Adult Survivors of Childhood Sexual Violation

This 'Heart Encounter' is a guided visualisation for adults to make peace with their younger self.

THIS GUIDED VISUALISATION PRODUCTION MAY HELP YOU TO IMAGINE MEETING THE INNER CHILD WITHIN YOU. HYPNOSIS OR GUIDED VISUALISATION IS NOT LIKE SLEEP. IT IS A DEEP RELAXATION TO HELP YOU CONNECT WITH YOUR INNER SELF NO MATTER WHAT AGE. CHANGES MAY OCCUR WITHIN YOU THAT WILL BE POSITIVE AND RELEASING, A BIT LIKE A DREAM.

SO FOR NOW, FIND A PLACE WHERE YOU WON'T BE DISTURBED AND JUST RELAX TAKING SOME DEEP BREATHS THROUGH YOUR NOSE, DEEP DOWN INTO YOUR STOMACH – GENTLY ALLOWING THAT BREATH TO COME OUT THROUGH YOUR MOUTH.

ALL YOU NEED TO DO IS RELAX AND LET THE SOUNDS DRIFT OVER YOU, GET YOURSELF COMFORTABLE WITH AS LOOSELY FITTING CLOTHING AS POSSIBLE AND JUST RELAX, YOU HAVE GIVEN THIS TIME FOR YOU TO JUST BE...SO THAT'S IT, JUST BE...

MAKING YOURSELF COMFORTABLE WILL GIVE YOU ALL THE RIGHT REASONS TO PAY ATTENTION TO YOUR BREATHING.

WHEN YOU HAVE FINISHED LISTENING TO THIS WHETHER THIS IS IN THE DAY OR BEFORE YOU GO TO SLEEP, YOU WILL AWAKEN SLOWLY WITH A SENSE OF INNER CALM AND FREEDOM FROM ANY STRESS. SO NOW, NOTICE YOUR BREATHING (SPEECH SLOWING) – THE SOFT IN AND OUT THAT NATURALLY AND INSTINCTIVELY HAPPENS ALL BY ITSELF. AND, AS YOU RELAX, TAKE SOME DEEPER BREATHS. GENTLY BREATHING IN AND GENTLY BREATHING OUT – ALL IS SAFE AND ALL IS CALM.

(SPEECH SLOWING)

AND...AS YOU FOCUS YOUR ATTENTION ON YOUR BREATHING, LET THAT SAFE AND CALM STAY WITH YOU AS YOU RELAX DEEPER AND DEEPER DOWN.

NOW WITH YOUR EYES CLOSED, START TO COUNT BACKWARDS – NOW – FROM 700.

699...698...697...(SLOWING)...696...695...694...THAT'S RIGHT ...693... COUNTING BACKWARDS ...692... ONLY AS SLOWLY AS ...691... YOU MIGHT THINK ABOUT RELAXING THE TINY MUSCLES AND SKIN ON YOUR FACE, NECK AND EYES, LET ANY FROWN OR PAINFUL MEMORIES HELD IN THOSE FOREHEAD MUSCLES LEAVE YOUR FACE NOW AND SMILE INTO THE WARMTH OF THIS RELAXATION AND PEACE...AS YOU BECOME COMFORTABLY (SLOWING) AWARE OF YOUR BODY FLOATING SAFELY AND PEACEFULLY, FREE AND RELEASED... AWARE OF YOUR CHEST...AND LEGS...AND CONTENTEDLY AWARE OF YOUR FEET...

AND FEEL YOUR SHOULDERS RELAX...DEEP DOWN INTO YOUR ARMS, DEEPLY RELAXING YOUR HANDS AND FINGERS...AS YOU GO DEEPER INTO...A GLORIOUS RELAXED DREAM STATE, A PLACE WHERE YOU CAN BE FREE, WHERE YOU CAN BE YOU, REMEMBERING TIMES WHEN YOU WERE YOUNG. A TIME WHEN YOU MAY HAVE BEEN HAPPY, MAYBE ON A SWING OR AT SCHOOL OR SOMEWHERE WITH SOMEONE SAFE, BREATHE

DEEPLY IN AND OUT AS YOUR MIND CAPTURES THAT IMAGE EVEN IF IT WAS JUST A SHORT TIME AND FOR NOW RELAX IN THE GENTLE CALM OF PEACE...

NOT EVEN THINKING ABOUT ANYTHING NOW – JUST ALLOW YOURSELF TO SINK DEEPER AND DEEPER.

DEEPER AND DEEPER...TOWARDS YOUR OWN PEACEFUL, INNER QUIETNESS. LET YOUR BREATHING CARRY ON IN ITS OWN GENTLE WAY AS YOU SENSE IT ON ITS OWN, DOING ITS OWN THING AS IT ALWAYS DOES AND ALWAYS HAS.

JUST RELAX, JUST DETACH AND BE FREE AS YOU DEEPEN YOUR RELAXATION EVEN MORE...AND – AS A CALMNESS DEEPLY TAKES OVER YOU – JUST KEEP NOTICING YOUR BREATHING...NOTICE HOW YOU FEEL YOURSELF SINKING DEEPER DOWN EVERY TIME YOU EXHALE...

YOUR BODY NEEDS TO BE COMPLETELY RELAXED TO LET THE NEW SENSE OF FREEDOM FLOW OVER AND AROUND YOU, SO YOU CAN START TO DO THIS BY RELAXING ALL OF YOUR MUSCLES AND LETTING GO OF TIGHTNESS OR ANY PAIN IN YOUR HEAD OR NECK – LOOSEN ANY TENSE FACIAL MUSCLES ESPECIALLY IN YOUR JAW – RELAXING YOUR EYES DEEPER AND DEEPER UNTIL THEY ARE SO RELAXED THAT YOUR FEELING OF LETTING GO BECOMES EVEN MORE REAL AND EVEN MORE SAFE. LET THIS FEELING OF COMPLETE AND UTTER FREEDOM AND SAFETY CASCADE DOWN DEEPER AND DEEPER DOWN INTO THE SOFTENED LINING OF YOUR THROAT AS IT SPIRALS AND LOOSENS THE TENSIONS AROUND YOUR SHOULDERS AND LIFTING THE WEIGHT AND BURDEN THAT YOU HAVE CARRIED THERE FOR SO LONG, FREE THEM OFF NOW – RELEASE THAT TENSION AND JUST LET IT GO – YOU DON'T NEED THAT ANY MORE – SENSE THE SAME RELAXED AND REJUVENATED FEELINGS WORK THEIR WAY DOWN THROUGH YOUR ARMS, WRISTS AND DEEP

INTO THE VERY ENDS OF YOUR FINGERTIPS, TINGLING, WARMING AS A NEW AND STRONG SENSE OF ENERGY BEGINS TO EMERGE, RELAXING YOU MORE AND MORE IN EVERY WAY AND EVERY TIME YOU HEAR THE WORD 'DOWN' THIS ONLY DEEPENS YOUR LEVEL OF PEACE AND SERENITY MORE...LET THIS FEELING OF COMPLETE AND UTTER FREEDOM THROUGHOUT YOUR BODY WORK ITS WAY DOWN AND DOWN DEEPER INTO YOUR CHEST, SOOTHING AS IT DOES, PASSING DOWN IN AND WEAVING AROUND YOUR HEART, YOUR LOVING AND AMAZING HEART – AND AS IT DOES, LET GO OF ALL PAIN IN YOUR HEART, PAIN FOR YOURSELF, YOU DON'T NEED IT ANY MORE YOU ARE ABOUT TO BE FREE OF IT – STAY RELAXED AND CALM AND LET THIS FEELING RESTORE YOU MORE AND MORE AS IT DRIFTS DOWN AND DOWN THROUGH YOUR ENTIRE BODY – RELAXING EVERY PART OF YOU, DEEPER AND DEEPER DOWN THROUGH YOUR HIPS – YOUR PELVIC AREA THE PART YOU MOSTLY AVOID TALKING OR THINKING ABOUT – JUST RELAX AND FEEL THE NEW SENSE OF FREEDOM AND SAFETY AS IT SINKS DOWN, DEEPER DOWN THROUGH THE TOPS OF YOUR LEGS, RELAXING YOU MORE AND MORE AS IT FLOWS BEAUTIFUL RELAXING RESTORATIVE ENERGY DOWN INTO YOUR THIGHS, FILLING EVERY MUSCLE – SOOTHING YOUR KNEES, IN FRONT AND BEHIND, DOWN THROUGH YOUR CALF MUSCLES, LOOSENING UP ANY TENSION IN YOUR ANKLES AND ALL THROUGH THOSE TINY LITTLE BONES IN YOUR FEET, DEEP DOWN INTO YOUR TOES – FEEL YOUR ENTIRE BODY RELAXED AND PEACEFUL DEEPER AND DEEPER DOWN INTO TRANQUIL HARMONY AS YOUR MIND AND BODY BECOME ONE.

OKAY SO NOW, WITH YOUR BODY AS COMFORTABLE AS POSSIBLE...AND FROM THE TOP OF YOUR HEAD IMAGINE A SPECIAL RELAXING AND WARMING RAY OF SUNSHINE IS SHINING DOWN ON YOU...SPIRALLING

THROUGH YOU...SPARKLING THROUGH YOUR BODY SLOWLY, TINGLING AS IT SHINES DOWN THROUGH YOU, AS YOUR BODY WARMS TO IT – STAYING RELAXED NOW.... YOU ARE IN COMPLETE CONTROL OF YOUR BODY AND OF YOUR MIND AS YOU ALLOW THIS BEAUTIFUL HEALING RAY OF SUNSHINE TO PROTECT AND NOURISH YOUR ENERGY BIT BY BIT...IMAGINE THE WARMTH OF THIS RAY OF SUNSHINE ON YOUR HEAD BEAMING DOWN...BRUSHING GENTLY ACROSS YOUR FACE MAKING YOU SMILE AT THE SOFTNESS OF IT....

AND AS IT CONTINUES TO GENTLY RELAX YOU DEEPER AND DEEPER ...NOW LET THIS RAY OF SUNSHINE CONTINUE TO EMBRACE YOU AS YOU ALLOW THE NATURAL WARMTH OF IT TO SOOTHE DEEP INTO YOUR SOUL...LIKE A LIQUID BALM....ALL OF YOUR PAIN AND PAST HURT...AS YOU LET IT GO...THIS SOOTHING, HEALING RAY CONTINUES TO EMBRACE AS IT MOVES DOWN THROUGH YOUR NECK AND SHOULDERS...AND DEEP INTO YOUR STOMACH, YOUR ABDOMEN...

RELAXING ALL OF YOUR MUSCLES GENTLY AND CALMLY, ALLOWING YOUR BREATHING TO JUST CARRY ON ALL BY ITSELF...THE RAY KEEPS FLOWING DOWN, SWIRLING, BEAUTIFUL AND WARM FURTHER DOWN NOW, THROUGH AND AROUND YOUR ARMS....YOUR HANDS AND THE TIPS OF YOUR FINGERS AS IT RELAXES EACH BONE, EACH MUSCLE EACH PORE OF SKIN ...INTO YOUR LEGS, KNEES AND CALVES RELAXING YOU EVEN MORE AND FINALLY SWIRLING AND HEALING INTO YOUR FEET AND TOES...

OKAY SO NOW, YOUR BODY IS EVEN MORE RELAXED... AND JUST FOR A MOMENT IMAGINE THAT YOU ARE COMPLETELY WEIGHTLESS FLOATING – THINKING GENTLY AS A WARM SOFT BREEZE BLOWS, COOLS AND COMFORTS YOU AND WHEREVER YOU ARE, YOU ARE COMPLETELY SAFE AND PROTECTED, IT CAN BE

SOMEWHERE YOU KNOW IN A BEAUTIFUL FOREST, ON A BEACH OR WHEREVER YOU FEEL IS RIGHT FOR YOU…

NOW IMAGINE THAT YOU ARE LOOKING UP INTO THE SKY…THINKING OF TIMES IN YOUR PAST WHEN YOU WERE RELAXED…NO PLANS…NO WORRIES… FEELING REALLY GOOD ABOUT YOURSELF…AND WHILE YOU ARE HERE LISTENING AND RELAXED, SAFE AND PROTECTED, JUST LET YOUR MIND DRIFT BACK IN TIME…BACK INTO THOSE YOUNGER DAYS WHEN YOU WERE SO MUCH SMALLER, WHEN EVERYONE ELSE MADE CHOICES FOR YOU, TOLD YOU WHAT WAS RIGHT AND WHAT WAS WRONG – WHETHER IT WAS OR NOT… LOOKING BACK INTO THE YEARS THAT HAVE GONE… ALL THE WAY BACK TO YOUR OWN CHILDHOOD, ALL THE LOSSES, ALL THE CHANGES, NEW FRIENDS, NEW SCHOOLS, GOOD TIMES, BAD TIMES, ENDLESS LAUGHTER AND ENDLESS TEARS…EVERYTHING WAS NEW TO YOU CHANGING SCHOOLS, TEACHERS, ALL CONFUSING AND NEW AND THEN LEAVING SCHOOL AND STARTING WORK OR COLLEGE OR UNIVERSITY ALL NEW AGAIN AND ALL STRANGE AT FIRST. ALL THOSE NEW EXPERIENCES IN YOUR YOUNGER LIFE…

(PAUSE) – NOW IMAGINE OR NOTICE AN OLD WOODEN COAT STAND AHEAD OF YOU – HANGING ON IT IS A PATCHWORK VELVET CAPE – NOTICE THE COLOUR – IT'S YOURS SO PUT IT ON, NOTICE ITS LIGHTNESS, THE COLLAR IS SOFT AND COMFORTABLE AND THE PATCHES ON IT REPRESENT ANY AND ALL OF THE PAST HURTS, YOU HAVE SUFFERED AS A CHILD – ASSAULTS, PHYSICAL AND SEXUAL ATTACKS, PAIN, BOTH PSYCHOLOGICAL AND PHYSICAL AND OLD, OLD STUFF THAT OTHER PEOPLE HAVE DONE TO YOU AGAINST YOUR WILL IN ORDER TO MEET THEIR OWN NEEDS.

EACH PATCH HOLDS ITS OWN STORY – ONLY YOU KNOW THOSE STORIES – SO YOU CHOOSE HOW MANY PATCHES THERE ON THIS VELVET RECOVERY CAPE.

OKAY, SO NOW YOU HAVE THE CAPE AROUND YOU –
BE READY TO DESCEND DOWN A BEAUTIFUL STAIRWAY
– RIGHT NOW YOU ARE STANDING AT THE TOP – IT
CAN SPIRAL OR STRAIGHT OR HOWEVER YOU WOULD
LIKE IT TO BE…MADE OF MARBLE, GNARLED WOOD,
ORNATE IRON RAILINGS, IT DOES NOT MATTER – IT'S
YOUR STAIRWAY AND YOU CAN DESIGN IT HOWEVER
YOU WANT TO….AND AS YOU RELAX IN THIS BEAUTIFUL
CALMNESS, COUNT YOURSELF DOWN THIS STAIRWAY
– EACH STEP REPRESENTING A NUMBER AND I WILL
COUNT THEM FOR YOU AS YOU GO DOWN.

10

9 DEEPER DOWN

8

7 FEELING LIGHTER AS YOU GO DOWN

6

5

4 DEEPER AND DEEPER

3

2

AND

1

NOW YOU ARE AT THE BOTTOM IN YOUR WEIGHTLESS
STATE OF MIND, FREE AND SAFE, SITTING, STANDING
WHEREVER YOU WANT TO BE, THINKING, REFLECTING
AND RELEASING THE OLD STUFF…

SCROLLING BACK THROUGH THOSE YEARS JUST LET
YOUR MIND TAKE YOU TO AN AGE AND TIME THAT YOU
WOULD MOST LIKE TO FORGET AND WHEN YOU ARRIVE
AT THAT AGE, THINK ABOUT THE PLACE WHERE YOU
WOULD GO, WHEN YOU NEEDED TO BE ON YOUR OWN
WHEN YOU WERE UNHAPPY, SCARED OR UNSAFE.

WAS IT YOUR BEDROOM,

THE STAIRS,

A CUPBOARD OR SHED OR SOMEWHERE ELSE?

REMEMBER THAT PLACE…
WHAT WAS THAT PLACE LIKE?
BUILD A PICTURE FOR YOURSELF
THINK ABOUT THE WALLPAPER, THE COLOUR,
ANY FURNITURE,
CARPETS,
A WINDOW

IF THERE IS ONE, WHAT COULD YOU SEE FROM THAT WINDOW…YOUR POSITION?

SEE YOURSELF AS THAT YOUNGER PERSON, WHAT ARE YOU WEARING? *(PAUSE FOR A FEW SECONDS TO ALLOW THOUGHT)*

OKAY AND NOW JUST SEE YOURSELF THERE AT THAT AGE, THINKING ABOUT ALL THE THINGS THAT HAPPENED OR WERE HAPPENING AT THAT TIME, FEELING ALL THOSE FEELINGS JUST AS YOU DID THEN. BRING THAT MEMORY BACK RIGHT NOW AND AS YOU DO THAT – YOU AS THE ADULT YOU ARE TODAY – BE THERE IN THAT PLACE WITH YOUR YOUNGER YOU – WHATEVER HAPPENED TO YOU – YOU MADE IT THROUGH BECAUSE YOU ARE STRONG, YOU SURVIVED – AND YOU ARE A WISER ADULT (STRONGER THAN YOU WILL EVER KNOW).

YOU HAVE GROWN UP…SO NOW GENTLY AND SOFTLY WALK OVER TO YOUR YOUNGER YOU TAKE HIS/HER HAND AND FIND SOMEWHERE SAFE AND THEN SIT DOWN BESIDE HIM/HER.

PUT YOUR ARMS TIGHTLY AROUND HIM/HER, HOLDING ON WITH LOVE AND KINDNESS RADIATING FROM YOUR OWN HEART AND PURE SOUL, NOW TELL THAT YOUNGER YOU THAT EVERYTHING IS GOING TO BE OKAY, TELL HIM/HER THAT THE STRENGTH IN HIM/HER WILL GET HIM/HER THROUGH THIS HORROR AND HE/SHE WILL BE OKAY – LOOK AT YOU BOTH THERE IN THE REFLECTION OF THE BIG BEAUTIFUL

MIRROR BEFORE YOU – YOUR YOUNGER YOU SO MUCH SMALLER AND YOU NOW SO MUCH OLDER AND WISER – WATCH THE TWO OF YOU AS YOU KEEP HOLDING ON, LOVING, EVEN HOLDING ON SO TIGHT THAT YOU CAN IMAGINE PULLING YOUR YOUNGER YOU BACK INSIDE WHERE HE/SHE REALLY BELONGS – AND YOU CAN TAKE YOUR YOUNGER YOU WITHIN YOU SO DEEPLY SO THAT HE/SHE BECOME PART OF YOU, WHERE HE/SHE WILL SHINE WITH YOU, WHERE HE/SHE WILL BE SAFE AND PROTECTED IN EVERYTHING YOU DO, AND EVERYTHING YOU SAY, FROM THIS DAY FORWARD – YOU ARE COMPLETELY IN CHARGE OF YOU BOTH NOW – IT'S YOUR VOICE THAT KEEPS HIM/HER SAFE BECAUSE YOUR YOUNGER YOU HAS BEEN OUTSIDE FOR A LONG TIME AND IT'S NOW TIME FOR YOU TO TAKE CARE OF THAT LITTLE ONE AND ALLOW THE BLENDING OF YOU NOW AS AN ADULT AND YOUR YOUNGER YOU AS A CHILD – YOU DESERVE TO BE FREE AND HAPPY JUST AS YOUR YOUNGER YOU DOES – TOGETHER NOW AS ONE… FOR ALWAYS.

YOU CAN RELAX NOW AND BE FREE AS WE REMEMBER WHEN YOU FIRST CAME DOWN THE BEAUTIFUL STAIRWAY CHOSEN BY YOU, YOU PUT ON THE VELVET CAPE…WELL NOW YOU CAN TAKE IT OFF AND LET IT FALL AWAY FROM YOU AND YOUR YOUNGER YOU. AND AS IT FALLS WATCH IT AS IT STARTS TO MELT INTO NOTHINGNESS AND YOU NOTICE EACH CORNER OF EACH PATCH SLOWLY MELTING AS IT BECOMES ONE BIG DISSOLVING NOTHINGNESS.

AS ALL THE PATCHES ON IT THAT REPRESENTED ALL OF YOUR PAST SADNESS, ASSAULTS, PHYSICAL AND SEXUAL ATTACKS, PAIN, PSYCHOLOGICAL AND PHYSICAL AND OLD, OLD STUFF FADE AWAY TO NOTHING, TO INSIGNIFICANCE –

AND TAKE A COUPLE OF REALLY DEEP BREATHS NOW ALL THE WAY IN AND ALL THE WAY OUT

ACKNOWLEDGING HOW FAR YOU HAVE COME – TO HAVE FACED THAT PAIN AND NOW YOU ARE FREE – COMPLETELY FREE…YOU ALONE HAVE FACED SO MUCH, YOU HAVE WALKED AWAY FROM THOSE PEOPLE WHO HURT YOU WITH NO REASON – AND IT'S YOUR TIME AND YOUR TURN TO BE FREE NOW – YOU HAVE A RIGHT TO BE FREE AND TO LIVE YOUR LIFE IN A WAY THAT SUITS YOU – NOT ANYONE ELSE AS YOU TAKE CARE OF YOU AND OF YOUR YOUNGER YOU, BECAUSE YOU ARE BLENDING AS ONE – SAFE AND PROTECTED.

AND SO NOW YOU ARE LIBERATED AND ABLE TO MOVE FORWARD WITH A NEW SENSE OF THE REAL YOU EMERGING DAY BY DAY – NEW IDEAS – NEW POSITIVE WAYS TO LIVE YOUR LIFE AND NOT BE HELD BACK OR CONTROLLED BY ANYONES ELSE'S THOUGHTS OR NEEDS – NO, JUST YOUR OWN.

IT REALLY IS YOUR TURN TO BE HAPPY NOW THAT YOU'VE LET GO OF ALL THAT MADE YOU SO SAD, NOW YOU WILL ONLY FEEL JOY AND EXCITEMENT AT THE NEW THINGS YOU WILL PLAN – ANYTHING THAT YOU PLAN YOU WILL MAKE HAPPEN BECAUSE IT WILL BE YOUR CHOICE AND YOUR CHOICE ALONE.

AND AS YOU STAY DEEPER AND DEEPER INTO RELAXATION WITH THE YOUNGER YOU SAFE AND SOUND DEEP WITHIN YOU AS YOU CONTINUE TO RELAX NOW AND STAY DEEPER AND DEEPER…ENJOYING THAT BEAUTIFUL PLACE OF RELAXATION… EMBRACE HAPPINESS AND LAUGHTER – TAKE IT – ABSORB IT FROM THE YOUNGER YOU WITHIN…WE ARE ALL UNIQUE AND HAVE VERY DIFFERENT WAYS OF BEING – LIKE PEBBLES ON A BEACH WE MAY LOOK SIMILAR BUT EACH HAS OUR OWN STORY – ALL DIFFERENT FROM EACH OTHER.

SO NOW YOU CAN BECOME THAT PERSON THAT YOU HAVE NEVER HAD THE CHANCE TO LET BE.

TAKE A FEW MOMENTS TO ENJOY AND EMBRACE THE NEW BLENDED HEART OF YOU AND YOUR YOUNGER YOU AS YOU RELAX AND ENJOY THE MOMENT, THE LAST SEALING OF THAT ETERNAL BOND.

YOU HAVE COME SO FAR – LIKE A WARRIOR YOU HAVE FACED THE WORST AND ARE STILL HERE – YOU ARE STILL HERE BECAUSE OF YOUR STRENGTH AND COURAGE AND YOUR PURE HEART. IT'S TIME NOW TO COME BACK TO YOUR LIFE MORE ENERGISED AND WITH YOUR YOUNGER YOU INSIDE SAFE AND PROTECTED AND REMEMBERING THAT BEAUTIFUL STAIRWAY THAT YOU CAME DOWN – IT'S TIME TO GO BACK UP SO, USING EACH STEP AS A NUMBER YOU WILL GRADULLY BECOME...MORE AND MORE BACK TO A SENSE OF CALM AND SAFETY.

ONE...

TWO GRADUALLY...STIRRING...

THREE...FEELING...SO REFRESHED...

FOUR...FIVE...SIX...

SEVEN...FEELING GREAT...EIGHT...

NINE...OPENING YOUR EYES NOW AND...

TEN...AWAKE AND AWARE.

This guided visualisation is available to purchase in Audio CD and MP3 Format from www.traumaresources.co.uk.

Specific Guided Visualisation for Those Affected by Rape and Sexual Violence

THE SPLINTER

THIS GUIDED VISUALISATION MAY HELP TO ASSIST WITH WORKING THROUGH THE TRAUMA OF BEING RAPED OR SEXUALLY ASSAULTED.

GUIDED VISUALISATION IS NOT LIKE SLEEP IT IS A DEEP RELAXATION TO HELP YOU CONNECT WITH YOUR SUBCONSCIOUS – A BIT LIKE HAVING A BEAUTIFUL STORY READ TO YOU, WHERE YOU SIMPLY FOLLOW IT IN YOUR OWN MIND.

YOU WON'T BECOME UNCONSCIOUS OR BE ASKED TO DO ANYTHING AGAINST YOUR WILL. OFTEN CHANGES MAY OCCUR WITHIN YOU THAT WILL BE POSITIVE AND RELEASING, A BIT LIKE A DREAM.

SO FOR NOW, FIND A PLACE WHERE YOU WON'T BE DISTURBED AND JUST RELAX TAKING SOME DEEP BREATHS THROUGH YOUR NOSE, DEEP DOWN INTO YOUR STOMACH – GENTLY RELEASING THAT BREATH OUT THROUGH YOUR MOUTH.

ALL YOU NEED TO DO IS RELAX AND LET THE SOUNDS DRIFT OVER YOU, GET YOURSELF COMFORTABLE WITH AS LOOSELY FITTING CLOTHING AS POSSIBLE AND JUST RELAX, YOU HAVE GIVEN YOURSELF THIS TIME FOR YOU TO JUST BE…SO THAT'S IT NOW…JUST BE…

MAKING YOURSELF COMFORTABLE WILL GIVE YOU ALL THE RIGHT REASONS TO PAY ATTENTION TO YOUR BREATHING.

WHEN YOU HAVE FINISHED LISTENING TO THIS GUIDED VISUALISATION, WHETHER THIS IS IN THE DAY OR BEFORE YOU GO TO SLEEP, YOU WILL AWAKEN SLOWLY WITH A SENSE OF INNER CALM AND FREEDOM FROM ANY STRESS. SO NOW, NOTICE YOUR BREATHING (SPEECH SLOWING) – THE SOFT IN AND OUT THAT NATURALLY AND INSTINCTIVELY HAPPENS ALL BY ITSELF. AND, AS YOU RELAX, TAKE SOME DEEPER BREATHS. GENTLY BREATHING IN AND GENTLY BREATHING OUT – ALL IS SAFE AND ALL IS CALM.

(SPEECH SLOWING)

AND...AS YOU FOCUS YOUR ATTENTION ON YOUR BREATHING,

LET THAT SAFE AND CALM STAY WITH YOU AS YOU RELAX DEEPER AND DEEPER DOWN

NOW WITH YOUR EYES CLOSED, START TO COUNT BACKWARDS – NOW – FROM 700.

699...698...697...(SLOWING)...696...695...694...THAT'S RIGHT ...693... COUNTING BACKWARDS ...692... ONLY AS SLOWLY AS ...691...YOU MIGHT THINK ABOUT RELAXING THE TINY MUSCLES AND SKIN ON YOUR FACE, NECK AND EYES, LET ANY FROWN OR PAINFUL MEMORIES HELD IN THOSE FOREHEAD MUSCLES LEAVE YOUR FACE NOW AND SMILE INTO THE WARMTH OF THIS RELAXATION AND PEACE...AS YOU BECOME COMFORTABLY (SLOWING) AWARE OF YOUR BODY FLOATING SAFELY AND PEACEFULLY, FREE AND RELEASED...AWARE OF YOUR WHOLE BODY, YOUR CHEST...AND LEGS...AND CONTENTEDLY AWARE OF YOUR FEET...

AND FEEL YOUR SHOULDERS RELAX...DEEP DOWN INTO YOUR ARMS, DEEPLY RELAXING YOUR HANDS AND FINGERS...AS YOU GO DEEPER INTO...A GLORIOUS RELAXED DREAM STATE, A PLACE WHERE YOU CAN BE

FREE, WHERE YOU CAN BE YOU, REMEMBERING TIMES WHEN YOU WERE YOUNG.

A TIME WHEN YOU MAY HAVE BEEN HAPPY, MAYBE ON A SWING OR AT SCHOOL OR SOMEWHERE WITH SOMEONE SAFE, BREATHE DEEPLY IN AND OUT, AS YOUR MIND CAPTURES THAT IMAGE EVEN IF IT WAS JUST A SHORT TIME AND FOR NOW RELAX IN THE GENTLE CALM OF PEACE...

NOT EVEN THINKING ABOUT ANYTHING NOW – JUST ALLOW YOURSELF TO SINK DEEPER AND DEEPER.

DEEPER AND DEEPER...TOWARDS YOUR OWN PEACEFUL, INNER QUIETNESS. LET YOUR BREATHING CARRY ON IN ITS OWN GENTLE WAY, DOING ITS OWN THING AS IT ALWAYS DOES AND ALWAYS HAS.

JUST RELAX, JUST DETACH AND BE FREE AS YOU DEEPEN YOUR RELAXATION EVEN MORE...AND –

AS A CALMNESS DEEPLY TAKES OVER YOU – JUST KEEP NOTICING YOUR BREATHING...NOTICE HOW YOU FEEL YOURSELF SINKING DEEPER DOWN EVERY TIME YOU EXHALE...

YOUR BODY NEEDS TO BE COMPLETELY RELAXED TO LET A NEW SENSE OF FREEDOM FLOW OVER AND AROUND YOU, SO NOW, YOU CAN START TO DO THIS BY RELAXING ALL OF YOUR MUSCLES AND LETTING GO OF TIGHTNESS OR ANY PAIN IN YOUR HEAD OR NECK – LOOSEN ANY TENSE FACIAL MUSCLES ESPECIALLY IN YOUR JAW – RELAX YOUR EYES AND GO DEEPER AND DEEPER UNTIL THEY ARE SO RELAXED THAT YOUR FEELING OF LETTING GO BECOMES EVEN MORE REAL AND EVEN MORE SAFE. LET THIS FEELING OF COMPLETE AND UTTER FREEDOM AND SAFETY CASCADE DOWN DEEPER AND DEEPER DOWN INTO THE SOFTENED LINING OF YOUR THROAT, AS IT SPIRALS AND LOOSENS THE TENSIONS AROUND YOUR SHOULDERS AND LIFTING THE WEIGHT AND BURDEN THAT YOU HAVE CARRIED THERE FOR SO LONG,

LOOSEN AND RELEASE THAT TENSION AND JUST LET IT GO – YOU DON'T NEED THAT ANY MORE – SENSE THE SAME RELAXED AND INVIGORATED FEELINGS WORK THEIR WAY DOWN THROUGH YOUR ARMS, WRISTS AND DEEP INTO THE VERY ENDS OF YOUR FINGERTIPS, TINGLING, WARMING AS A NEW AND STRONG SENSE OF ENERGY BEGINS TO EMERGE, RELAXING YOU MORE AND MORE IN EVERY WAY AND EVERY TIME YOU HEAR THE WORD 'DOWN' THIS ONLY DEEPENS YOUR LEVEL OF PEACE AND SERENITY EVEN MORE...LET THIS FEELING OF COMPLETE AND UTTER FREEDOM THROUGHOUT YOUR BODY WORK ITS WAY DOWN AND DOWN DEEPER INTO YOUR CHEST, SOOTHING AS IT DOES, PASSING DOWN IN AND WEAVING AROUND YOUR HEART, YOUR LOVING AND AMAZING HEART – AND AS IT DOES, LET GO OF ALL PAIN IN YOUR HEART, PAIN FOR YOURSELF, YOU JUST DON'T NEED IT ANYMORE YOU ARE ABOUT TO BE FREE OF IT – SO STAY RELAXED AND CALM AND LET THIS FEELING RESTORE YOU MORE AND MORE AS IT DRIFTS DOWN AND DOWN THROUGH YOUR ENTIRE BODY – RELAXING EVERY PART OF YOU,

DEEPER AND DEEPER DOWN THROUGH YOUR HIPS – YOUR PELVIC AREA THE PART YOU MOSTLY AVOID TALKING OR THINKING ABOUT – JUST RELAX AND FEEL THE NEW SENSE OF FREEDOM AND SAFETY AS IT SINKS DOWN, DEEPER DOWN THROUGH THE TOPS OF YOUR LEGS,

RELAXING YOU MORE AND MORE AS IT FLOWS BEAUTIFUL RELAXING RESTORATIVE ENERGY DOWN INTO YOUR THIGHS, FILLING EVERY MUSCLE – SOOTHING YOUR KNEES, IN FRONT AND BEHIND, DOWN THROUGH YOUR CALF MUSCLES, LOOSENING UP ANY TENSION IN YOUR ANKLES AND ALL THROUGH THOSE TINY LITTLE BONES IN YOUR FEET, DEEP DOWN INTO YOUR TOES – FEEL YOUR ENTIRE BODY RELAXED AND PEACEFUL DEEPER AND DEEPER DOWN

INTO TRANQUIL HARMONY AS YOUR MIND AND BODY BECOME ONE.

OKAY SO NOW, WITH YOUR BODY AS COMFORTABLE AS POSSIBLE...AND FROM THE TOP OF YOUR HEAD IMAGINE A SPECIAL RELAXING AND WARMING RAY OF SUNSHINE IS SHINING DOWN ON YOU... SPIRALLING THROUGH YOU...SPARKLING THROUGH YOUR BODY SLOWLY, TINGLING AS IT SHINES DOWN THROUGH YOU, AS YOUR BODY WARMS TO IT – STAYING RELAXED NOW...YOU ARE IN COMPLETE CONTROL OF YOUR BODY AND OF YOUR MIND AS YOU ALLOW THIS BEAUTIFUL HEALING RAY OF SUNSHINE TO PROTECT AND NOURISH YOUR ENERGY BIT BY BIT...IMAGINE THE WARMTH OF THIS RAY OF SUNSHINE ON YOUR HEAD BEAMING DOWN...BRUSHING GENTLY ACROSS YOUR FACE AND MAKING YOU SMILE AT THE SOFTNESS OF IT...

AND AS IT CONTINUES TO GENTLY RELAX YOU DEEPER AND DEEPER...NOW LET THIS RAY OF SUNSHINE CONTINUE TO EMBRACE YOU AS YOU ALLOW THE NATURAL WARMTH OF IT TO SOOTHE DEEP INTO YOUR SOUL...LIKE A LIQUID BALM...LET GO ALL OF YOUR PAIN AND PAST HURT...AS THIS RAY OF SUNSHINE STARTS TO HEAL YOU THROUGHOUT YOUR BODY...JUST LET IT GO...THIS SOOTHING, HEALING RAY CONTINUES TO EMBRACE AS IT MOVES DOWN THROUGH YOUR NECK AND SHOULDERS...AND DEEP INTO YOUR STOMACH, YOUR ABDOMEN...RELAXING ALL OF YOUR MUSCLES GENTLY AND CALMLY, ALLOWING YOUR BREATHING TO JUST CARRY ON ALL BY ITSELF...THE RAY KEEPS FLOWING DOWN, SWIRLING, BEAUTIFUL AND WARM FURTHER DOWN NOW, THROUGH AND AROUND YOUR ARMS...YOUR HANDS AND THE TIPS OF YOUR FINGERS AS IT RELAXES EACH BONE, EACH MUSCLE EACH PORE OF SKIN...INTO YOUR LEGS, KNEES AND CALVES RELAXING YOU EVEN MORE AND FINALLY CIRCLING AROUND AND HEALING INTO YOUR FEET AND TOES...

OKAY SO NOW, YOUR BODY IS EVEN MORE RELAXED...
AND JUST FOR A MOMENT IMAGINE THAT YOU ARE
COMPLETELY WEIGHTLESS, FLOATING – THINKING
GENTLY AS A WARM SOFT BREEZE BLOWS, COOLS
AND COMFORTS YOU AND WHEREVER YOU ARE, YOU
ARE COMPLETELY SAFE AND PROTECTED, IMAGINE
THAT YOU ARE STANDING AT THE TOP, LOOKING
DOWN A BEAUTIFUL STAIRWAY, AND YOU ARE READY
TO DESCEND RIGHT DOWN TO THE BOTTOM...SO
BE READY TO GO DOWN, NOW THIS STAIRWAY CAN
SPIRAL OR BE STRAIGHT OR HOWEVER YOU WOULD
LIKE IT TO BE...BUILT OF MARBLE, GNARLED WOOD,
ORNATE IRON RAILINGS IT DOES NOT MATTER, IT'S
YOUR STAIRWAY AND YOU CAN DESIGN IT HOWEVER
YOU WANT TO...AND AS YOU RELAX IN THIS BEAUTIFUL
CALMNESS, COUNT YOURSELF DOWN THIS STAIRWAY
WITH ME AS I COUNT – EACH STEP REPRESENTING A
NUMBER AS YOU GO DOWN

10

9 DEEPER DOWN

8

7 FEELING LIGHTER AS YOU GO DOWN

6

5

4 DEEPER AND DEEPER

3

2

AND

1

NOW YOU ARE AT THE BOTTOM IN YOUR WEIGHTLESS
STATE OF MIND, FREE AND SAFE, SITTING, STANDING
WHEREVER YOU WANT TO BE, THINKING, REFLECTING
AND RELEASING THE OLD STUFF...AND AS YOU DO SO
– IMAGINE OR SEE THAT JUST BEFORE YOU IS A LARGE

WOODEN RUSTIC TABLE WITH AN ANCIENT WOODEN CARVED CHAIR MADE FROM AN

OLD TREE STUMP – NOTICE THE WORN DOWN SHAPE WHERE MANY BEFORE YOU HAVE SAT AND WORKED THROUGH THEIR OWN INDIVIDUAL DIFFICULTIES...

TO THE LEFT OF YOU THERE IS AN OPEN FIRE PIT THAT HAS BURNED FOR CENTURIES AND IT CONTINUES TO BURN TO KEEP YOU WARM, COMFORTABLE AND SAFE...

AS YOU MAKE YOURSELF COMFORTABLE IN THE OLD WOODEN CHAIR BESIDE THIS LOVELY BURNING FIRE PIT – NOTICE A JIGSAW PUZZLE ON A WOODEN TABLE – THE PICTURE ON THE BOX IS AN IMAGE – AN IMAGE THAT ONLY YOU CAN SEE – THIS IMAGE REPRESENTS THE MOST DISTURBING PARTS OF THE TIME OR TIMES WHEN YOU WERE SEXUALLY ASSAULTED...

THERE ARE TWENTY-FOUR LARGE PIECES OF JIGSAW, AND... IN YOUR OWN TIME AND AS SLOWLY OR AS FAST AS YOU NEED TO... AND WITH THE COURAGE AND RESILIENCE THAT YOU HAVE ALREADY SHOWN TO HAVE EVEN GOT THIS FAR, START TO PUT THE PIECES OF THIS JIGSAW PUZZLE TOGETHER – YOU WILL NOTICE THAT IT FITS TOGETHER EASILY – YOU HAVE SEEN THIS PICTURE SO MANY TIMES IN YOUR HEAD.

SO NOW THE IMAGE OR MIXTURE OF IMAGES IS PRESENTED FULLY AND IT'S ALL PUT TOGETHER INTO A BIGGER PICTURE SO THAT YOU'RE LOOKING DOWN ON IT FROM ABOVE...JUST WATCH IT NOW FOR THE FIRST TIME IN A VERY DIFFERENT WAY – NOTICE AS THE COLOURS SLOWLY START TO FADE IN FRONT OF YOUR VERY EYES – WATCH THE ENERGY RUN OUT OF EACH AND EVERY PIECE OF THAT JIGSAW UNTIL ALL YOU CAN SEE BEFORE YOU IS A MUCH FAINTER IMAGE AND THAT IMAGE NOW FADES MORE AND MORE – IT HAS BECOME INSIGNIFICANT LIKE A WASHED OUT NEWSPAPER – NOW, YOU DON'T NEED TO LOOK AT THAT

IMAGE, THINK ABOUT OR SEE IT EVER AGAIN – SO JUST PULL THAT JIGSAW PUZZLE APART QUICKLY, BIT BY BIT AND THROW THEM ON TO THE OPEN PIT FIRE – YOU HAVE THE POWER NOW AS YOU WATCH EACH PIECE, EACH HURT, ALL THE JUDGEMENTS PEOPLE MAY HAVE MADE ABOUT YOU – ALL THE WRONGS THAT HAVE BEEN DONE UNTO YOU SINCE THE SEXUAL ATTACKS, SECONDARY INJURIES CAUSED BY OTHER AGENCIES OR PEOPLE'S INCOMPETENT ATTITUDES, ANY PAIN, JUST WATCH THEM ALL BURN AWAY IN THIS ENDLESS, ANCIENT FIRE, WHERE MANY OTHERS BEFORE YOU HAVE BURNED THEIR HURTS TOO…WATCH THE FIRE AS IT CHANGES COLOUR FROM GLOWING ORANGE TO THE DEEPEST RED AS IT DEVOURS THOSE JIGSAW PIECES INTO ASH…MELTING, BURNING AND FINALLY GONE… TAKE A DEEP BREATH AND SMELL THE WONDERFUL WOOD SMOKE AS THEY BURN, BURN, BURN AWAY – FOREVER GONE…..

SO CONTINUE TO JUST RELAX NOW FOR A FEW MOMENTS AS THE SOUNDS CONTINUE TO DRIFT OVER YOU SAFE AND SOUND IN THIS BEAUTIFUL PLACE OF CALM, PEACE AND FREEDOM. AND NOW…JUST TO MAKE ABSOLUTELY SURE THAT YOU HAVE GOT RID OF THAT IMAGE FROM NOT ONLY YOUR MIND BUT ALSO YOUR BODY – IMAGINE THAT ANY OTHER PAIN THAT MAY BE HELD IN YOUR BODY IS HELD IN JUST ONE PLACE – IN A 'TRAUMA SPLINTER®' – THIS SPLINTER CAN BE OF ANY MATERIAL – ONLY YOU KNOW IF IT FEELS MORE LIKE WOOD OR METAL OR EVEN GLASS OR SOMETHING DIFFERENT – YOU CHOOSE…

NOW…YOU WILL KNOW THAT THIS SPLINTER IS LODGED SOMEWHERE IN YOU – IT MIGHT BE IN YOUR SKIN OR DOWN BELOW, ONLY YOU KNOW WHERE IT IS… BECAUSE YOU HAVE HAD TO LIVE WITH IT…AND…A BIT LIKE THOSE SPLINTERS YOU USED TO GET AS A CHILD… IT HAS TO COME OUT OR IT WILL LEAD TO FURTHER

PROBLEMS...NOW YOU MIGHT OR MIGHT NOT KNOW THAT THE BEST WAY TO DRAW OUT A 'SPLINTER' IS A SMALL AMOUNT OF OLIVE OIL OR SOOTHING BALM AND WITH JUST A LITTLE BIT OF EFFORT ON YOUR PART THIS IS TRULY THE BEST WAY.

SO NOW THAT YOU HAVE DECIDED AND FOUND WHERE THE 'TRAUMA SPLINTER®' IS LODGED. IMAGINE THAT YOU START TO POUR SOME OIL OR BALM INTO THAT AREA...KEEP CONCENTRATING ON THAT AREA – YOU WILL BE ABLE TO SEE OR FEEL THE TOP OF THE 'TRAUMA SPLINTER®' BECAUSE IT WILL APPEAR – SLOWLY, SLOWLY AND VERY GENTLY IT WILL START TO MOVE – BECAUSE YOUR SUBCONSCIOUS KNOWS THAT IT'S TIME NOW FOR YOU TO LET OUT THE PAIN, ALL OF THOSE OTHER FEELINGS LIKE SHAME AND GUILT AND OLD, OLD FEELINGS AND EMOTIONS MANIFESTING IN YOUR BODY THAT YOU SIMPLY DON'T NEED ANY MORE...IT'S TIME TO GET RID OF IT ALL PROPERLY – TO REMOVE AND TO RELEASE THE PAIN YOU'VE BEEN GOING THROUGH AND PAIN THAT YOUR BODY HAS BEEN HANGING ON TO ALL THIS TIME...

NOW...AS THE 'TRAUMA SPLINTER®' IS ABOUT TO COME OUT – IT WILL DO SO GENTLY AND YOU WON'T FEEL ANY PAIN

...AND IT WILL BE QUICK...IT WILL JUST GLIDE OUT...ONTO THE GROUND OR FLOOR OF WHERE YOU ARE...SO, AFTER MY COUNT OF THREE, THE 'TRAUMA SPLINTER®' WILL JUST COME OUT BRINGING WITH IT ALL THE TOXIC FEELINGS, EMOTIONS HELD IN THE MUSCLES AND THE BODY PAIN THAT YOU HAVE BEEN GOING THROUGH ALL THIS TIME

IT WILL BE FAST WHEN IT HAPPENS...SO LETS COUNT TO THREE NOW

READY...

1

2

3

OH MY GOODNESS! FEEL THAT RELIEF AS THE 'TRAUMA SPLINTER®' IS FINALLY REMOVED FROM YOUR BODY – NOTICE THE EMPTY SPACE WHERE IT CAME FROM START TO CLOSE UP AND WATCH AS IT HEALS THAT PAINFUL PART OF YOUR SKIN SO QUICKLY, SO BEAUTIFULLY, SO PURE, SO THAT THE 'TRAUMA SPLINTER®' CAN NEVER EVER GO BACK IN NOW – IT'S GONE AND IT'S FINALLY OVER.

SO PICK IT UP AND DROP IT IN THE FIRE PIT AND WATCH AS IT MELTS AND BUBBLES AND BURNS AWAY INTO NOTHINGNESS – THAT TOTAL AND UTTER FREEDOM YOU NOW HAVE BEFORE YOU. NOTHING AND NO ONE WILL BE ABLE TO UNDO THE BRILLIANT WORK THAT YOU'VE DONE TODAY BECAUSE YOU ARE UNIQUE, YOU ARE COURAGEOUS BEYOND ALL DOUBT AND YOU CAN NOW LIVE YOUR LIFE WITHOUT FEAR OR PAIN AND LOVE THOSE WHO LOVE YOU BACK... JUST AS THOSE BEFORE YOU WHO HAVE VISITED THIS BEAUTIFUL PLACE, WHO HAVE LET GO OF THEIR PAIN AND SUFFERING AND MOVED ON TO LIVE BEAUTIFUL AND HAPPY LIVES JUST LIKE YOU ARE GOING TO DO FROM NOW ON...BECAUSE NOW YOU ARE FREE TO MOVE FORWARD WITH A NEW SENSE OF THE REAL YOU EMERGING DAY BY DAY – NEW IDEAS – NEW POSITIVE WAYS TO LIVE YOUR LIFE AND NOT BE HELD BACK OR CONTROLLED BY ANYONES ELSE'S THOUGHTS OR NEEDS – NO, JUST YOUR OWN. IT REALLY IS YOUR TURN TO BE HAPPY NOW THAT YOU'VE LET GO OF ALL THAT MADE YOU SO SAD, NOW YOU WILL ONLY FEEL JOY AND EXCITEMENT – ANYTHING THAT YOU PLAN YOU WILL MAKE HAPPEN BECAUSE IT WILL BE YOUR CHOICE AND YOUR CHOICE ALONE.

AND AS YOU STAY DEEPER AND DEEPER INTO RELAXATION YOU CONTINUE TO RELAX NOW AND STAY DEEPER AND DEEPER...ENJOYING THAT BEAUTIFUL PLACE OF RELAXATION... EMBRACE HAPPINESS AND LAUGHTER ...WE ARE ALL UNIQUE AND HAVE VERY DIFFERENT WAYS OF BEING – LIKE PEBBLES ON A BEACH WE MAY LOOK SIMILAR BUT EACH HAS OUR OWN STORY – ALL DIFFERENT FROM EACH OTHER SO NOW YOU CAN BECOME THAT PERSON THAT YOU HAVE NOT REALLY HAD THE CHANCE TO LET BE. FOR A WHILE TAKE A FEW MOMENTS TO ENJOY AND EMBRACE THE NEW YOU WITHOUT THE BURDEN OR WEIGHT OF THE OLD TRAUMA SPLINTER AS YOU RELAX AND ENJOY THE MOMENT, ENJOYING THE PEACE. IT'S TIME NOW TO COME BACK TO YOUR LIFE MORE ENERGISED REMEMBERING THE BEAUTIFUL STAIRWAY THAT YOU CAME DOWN – YOU WILL NOW RETURN BACK UP THE STEPS, SO, USING EACH STEP AS A NUMBER YOU WILL GRADULLY BECOME...MORE AND MORE BACK TO A SENSE OF CALM AND SAFETY

ONE...TWO   GRADUALLY...STIRRING...THREE... FEELING...

SO   REFRESHED...FOUR...FIVE...SIX...MORE   AND MORE ALIVE AND ALERT...SEVEN...FEELING GREAT... EIGHT...NINE...OPENING YOUR EYES NOW AND...TEN... RETURNING TO A NEW SENSE OF AWARENESS

This guided visualisation is available to purchase in Audio CD and MP3 format from www.traumaresources.co.uk

Appendix 8

Personal Healing and Recovery Plan

(Client name) . . . .

Foreword

Client's thoughts of their last ten years – bullet pointed list of significant events.

. . . .

. . . .

. . . .

. . . .

. . . .

Aims

One to five years – what you want and need to achieve to make your life better for you.

. . . .

. . . .

. . . .

. . . .

. . . .

Personal goals

Example:

Personal Goal
e.g. to cope better with what happened

Lead Responsibility	Me
Others with Role to play	Therapist, Support Worker, Rape Crisis

	Work to be undertaken	Timescale	Status
1a	To research and find suitable therapist or support that will enable me commit to my own healing & recovery.	1–10 months	ONG
1b			
1c			

Status – Key	
A	Achieved
NA	Not Achieved
PA	Partly Achieved
ONG	Ongoing

You can add as many pages of personal goals as the client requires.

Life Goals

Example:

Life Goal
To set up my own online business making cloth handbags.

Lead Responsibility	Me
Others with Role to play	Bank

	Work to be undertaken	Timescale	Status
2a	To research the market	12 months	NA
2b	To speak to my bank and discuss options	6 months	NA
2c			

Status – Key	
A	Achieved
NA	Not Achieved
PA	Partly Achieved
ONG	Ongoing

You can add as many pages of life goals as the client requires.

Full Plan

Full plan for the next ten years is...

These should be realistic dreams that you can make become actual facts.

. . . .

. . . .

. . . .

. . . .

. . . .

Stakeholders of my future plans and goals

e.g. Family, spouse, children, who and what I invest in

. . . .

. . . .

. . . .

. . . .

. . . .

Appendix 9

VK Dissociation, Phobia Cure or Rewind Technique

"The rewind technique, also known as the fast phobia cure, evolved from the technique developed by Richard Bandler, one of the co-founders of Neuro Linguistic Programming (NLP). He called it the VK dissociation technique (the V stands for visual and the K for kinaesthetic – feelings). The version recommended by the European Therapy Studies Institute has been refined and streamlined, as a result of its own research into why and how best it works. It is highly useful for individuals who, after exposure to traumatic events, have developed PTSD or lesser forms of the condition.

Simply described, the technique works by allowing the traumatised individual, whilst in a safe relaxed state, to reprocess the traumatic memory, so that it becomes stored as an 'ordinary', albeit unpleasant, and non-threatening memory rather than one that continually activates a terror response. This is achieved by enabling the memory to be shifted in the brain from the amygdala to the neocortex.

The amygdala's role is to alert us to danger and stimulate the body's 'fight or flight' reaction. Normally, all initial sensations associated with a threatening experience are passed to the amygdala and formed into a sensory memory, which in turn is passed on to the hippocampus and from there to the neocortex where it is translated into a verbal or narrative memory and stored. When an event appears life threatening, however, there can be sudden information overload and the sensory memories stay trapped in the amygdala instead of being passed on to, and made sense of by, the neocortex.

While trapped in the amygdala, the trauma memory has no identifiable meaning. It cannot be described, only re-experienced in some sensory form, such as panic attacks or flashbacks. The rewind technique allows that sensory memory to be converted into narrative, and be put into perspective. It is our sense that trauma is often seen within the mental health profession as a long-term problem and is perhaps more often misdiagnosed than diagnosed.

Rewind, however, puts a trauma into perspective very neatly. The treatment takes only a short time: perhaps close to the length of time the incident took to occur – a terrible experience but a tiny part of an entire life. By relocating the traumatic memory from one part of the brain to another – the place where it was meant to end up in the first place – it re-balances the experience within a person's life.

Most of the people we work with just want to put their experience into proper perspective, not suffer symptoms any more and get on with their lives. Rewind is not only powerfully effective in that respect but side effect free."

(Griffin and Tyrrell 2001)

There are a few different ways to use this intervention. The way we use it at Jigsaw is as follows:

First, explain to the client exactly what you would like them to do.
'Okay, Jane, I would like you to bring to the front of your mind your very own cinema with your very own screen. You are perfectly safe in this cinema, and you have full of control of everything in it. Can you do that?'

'Okay, now can you imagine that you have your own remote control, with three buttons that are labelled PLAY, STOP and REWIND. You can give the buttons colours if you want.'

Wait for the client to relate this information to you and the description so that you are sure they are involved.

'I'm going to ask you to give me a description of a moment five minutes before the traumatic incident occurred.'

So, for example, if a client had been raped, they would give you the moments they were walking up the street or laughing and chatting, as they were leaving their friend or similar.

'And can you give me a description of a time when the traumatic incident had finished – when you knew you were safe and out of harm's way?'

If the client had been raped, it may be when the rapist ran off, or when the police got there or when they arrived at the hospital or SARC. Let them tell you.

'So now we have a start and a finish, I will be asking you in a moment to close your eyes and play a film on your own screen in your own cinema (in your own head – you do not have to say anything out loud) of the traumatic incident from the five minutes before to the time when you knew you were safe – when you reach that point, keep your eyes closed and say the word STOP. I will be waiting for that moment, at which point I will then facilitate by saying, okay, now, Jane, imagine pressing the rewind button and rewind the film all the way back to the beginning of the five minutes before the traumatic incident occurred.'

'That's good. Now then, when you are ready, I would like you to take a deep breath in through your nose for the count of seven and out through your mouth for the count of eleven. Close your eyes and watch the film from scene to scene and take your time.'

If the client is willing to do this wait patiently, allowing them to go through their experience in their own time and at their own pace. You will see their eyes flickering under their eyelids, which is replicating the REM sleep process – our filing system – the only difference is that they are now processing information in the waking state. When they have followed instructions, rewound the traumatic incident and are back at the initial place before it happened, ask them to open their eyes and take a few seconds' breather.

This technique can sometimes be quite distressing, as they suddenly see the incident in complete sequence, and they may not have done this before. Ask them to do it one more time, but this time, when they get to the rewind part, ask them to make it black and white or sepia or whatever puts it in the past for them. When working with younger people, it's important to remember that the term 'black and white and/or sepia' may be trendy to them, and the idea is to put the incident as far back as they can. This is not normally a problem but it can happen.

When the client is 'back in the room' or when they open their eyes, ask them if they thought there was any difference between the first and the second time.
The answer you are looking for is something like 'It felt easier to do. It wasn't so difficult, painful or emotional.'

This will reveal to you that the impact has already lessened for the client. In addition to this, ask if they feel safe, to do exactly what they have just done, on their own at home, because the more they can do it the lesser the impact will be for them.

Appendix 10

Three Point Turnaround System© Approach to Working with Rape and Sexual Violence

The Three Point Turnaround System may take six weeks or sixty, depending on the expectation and immediate needs of the client and how you decide to work.

Point 1: initial assessment and sexual assault trauma timeline

Sexual Assault Timeline SAMPLE

Company or Organisational LOGO

*Company or Organisational Name and Address

Client details

Mr/Mrs/Miss/Ms/Other	Surname:
DOB/Age	First name:
Address:	
Telephone no:	Reference no.

Age

....

Age

....

Age

....

Age

....

Age

....

Age

....

Make specific notes regarding what the client believes are the worst moments for him/her.

Use the back of the sheets if preferable and if more room is needed.

....

....

....

....

....

....

....

Risk assessment

. . . .

. . . .

. . . .

. . . .

. . . .

Focus of work
Agreed focus of work – client states which part of their timeline that they would like to work on first

. . . .

. . . .

. . . .

. . . .

. . . .

Professional details:

Name:

Location of assessment:

Signature of Professional: Date of signature:

Point 2: processing intervention

Complete the chosen 'processing' intervention. There are several ways of working with a person who has been traumatised. Recognition that each client, service user or patient is unique and will respond differently is key in the initial stages of assistance. Therefore it is crucial to be able to identify which intervention will suit each individual (see 'Treatment matching' in Chapter 12, p.163). Keep notes on each session to allow a scale of progress throughout.

Point 3: evaluation of intervention and outcome for the client

Ask the client to work through his/her own evaluation with you. This is not about whether you as a professional have done a good job; it is about whether or not the client feels that they have achieved a level of recovery suitable to them.

The evaluation should be true and honest and as a professional you need to feel okay to signpost on to further work if the intervention delivered has not had any positive outcome for the client.

This evaluation is key to recovery and adaption, because many of those affected by sexual violation especially, although not always, have been conditioned to feel and react in a certain way and to move on can sometimes seem unreal and completely unmanageable.

By working with the client to allow their own measure of recovery, safely and in their own time without feeling rushed or under any pressure, we can nurture them as they begin to regain control of self, of choices and a new future they have chosen.

Client EVALUATION SAMPLE

Company or Organisational LOGO

*Company or Organisational Name and Address

Client details

Mr/Mrs/Miss/Ms/Other   Surname:

DOB/Age   First name:

Address:

Telephone no: Reference no.

Please rate the following aspects of the work you have undertaken in the three months, on a scale of 1 – 100%:

Initial Assessment and Sexual Assault Trauma Line 1 – 100%

. . . .

Ability to work productively and progressively 1 – 100%

. . . .

How much progress have you made towards recovery? 1 – 100%

. . . .

Please answer the following open questions to the best of your ability by being as open and as honest as possible.

What part of the work that you have undertaken has helped you the most and why?

. . . .
. . . .
. . . .

What part of the work, if any, did you find was not useful and why?

. . . .
. . . .
. . . .

Do you feel able to move on to a new part in your life, leaving the traumatic incidents of the past behind you?

. . . .
. . . .
. . . .

Is there anything else or other therapy that you feel you might need to additionally assist with your recovery and restoration into a new and fulfilling life?

. . . .

. . . .

. . . .

Is there anything else that you would like to add regarding the treatment and/or processing interventions that you have been given?

. . . .

. . . .

. . . .

Thank you for completing this evaluation – we can now work with how you move on.

Once you have the correct information from the client, between you, you are then able to ascertain the client's next move. You may be able to signpost to an organisation that can offer further assistance, which may be on a more practical level such as housing, safe living or possible work information.

Appendix 11

Example SOA 2003 Notification Requirement

Name . . . .

SOA 2003 NOTIFICATION REQUIREMENTS

(As amended by legislation August 2012)

A person required by the 2003 Act to register with the police is required by law to:

1. Notify the police within 3 days of the caution, conviction or finding (or, if he/she is in custody or otherwise detained, 3 days from his release) of his/her name, date of birth and home address at the time of the conviction, caution or finding. (*Section 83*)

In addition, he/she is also required to notify the police of their current name, including any aliases they use, and their sole or main residence in the United Kingdom or, if they have no such residence, any premises in the United Kingdom at which they can be found, if either are different from the name and address at the time of conviction.

2. Submit - on initial notification, on notification of any changes to registered details and on periodic notification - to having his/her fingerprints and photograph taken. (*Section 87(4)*)

3. Notify the police of any changes to the name and address he/she has registered **within 3 days of the date of any change**, including release from prison for subsequent offences. (*Section 84*)

4. Notify the police of any address where he/she resides or stays for 7 days or longer. This means either 7 days at a time, or a total of 7 days in any 12-month period. (*Section 84*)

5. Notify the police **weekly** where registered as 'no fixed abode'.

6. Notify the Police if he/she has resided or stayed for at least 12 hours at a household or other private place where an under 18 year old resides or stays.

7. Notify police of passport, all credit card, all debit card and all bank account details and certain information contained in a passport or other form of identification held by the relevant offender **on each notification and within 3 days of any changes to the detail**.

(ID MUST BE PROVIDED or you will be turned away)

8. All offenders must re-confirm their details **within one year** of their last notification. (*Section 85*)

9. All offenders have to notify their National Insurance Numbers on each notification. (*Section 83(5)*)

An offender can only give this notification by attending a police station prescribed for the purpose by regulations in the police area where they reside. (The regulations will be periodically updated when the addresses of police stations change).

New name and address: For advance notification if the change takes place more than two days before the anticipated date, the police must be informed. If an advance notification is made and the change has not taken place within three days beginning with the anticipated date, the police must be informed within six days of the anticipated date.

Appendix 12

Example Foreign Travel Notification

FOREIGN TRAVEL

Section 86 stipulates that offenders are required by law to notify the police no less than 7 days in advance of any intended period of foreign travel.

Foreign travel notifications must be made, at least 7 days before the anticipated date of departure where the information is held by the offender.

Where the information is not known 7 days before departure, the offender must give the foreign travel notification as soon as reasonably practicable but not less than 12 hours before that date, **if and only if** the relevant offender has a reasonable excuse for not complying with the seven day notification requirement.

The information which must be notified, includes;

1. The departure date,

2. The destination country/countries, including port of arrival,

3. Travel arrangements (carrier details, flight/ferry/ booking reference numbers);

4. The dates on which he intends to stay in any country to which he intends to travel;

5. Details of his accommodation arrangements in any country to which he intends to travel;

6. Expected date of return to UK and port of arrival.

Any changes to the detail provided, at any time, must be notified in person at a Police Station within 3 days of return to the UK.

Notifying intended foreign travel must also be completed at a prescribed police station in person. Foreign Travel notifications DO **NOT** alter the date of periodic notifications.

An offender who fails to comply with the notification requirements set out above, without reasonable excuse, or who provides the police with information which he or she knows to be false, could be sent to prison for up to 5 years.

I have received a copy of this form and been made aware of the penalty section.

I fully understand the terms of my Notification Requirements.

Signed . . . . *Dated* . . . .

Name: . . . .

Served by . . . . Police Force

Copy Taken: Yes / No

References

Donaldson, S. (1990) *Stephen Donaldson Papers*. New York: New York Public Library.

Finkelhor, D. (1980) 'Sex among siblings: A survey on prevalance, variety, and effects.' *Archives of Sexual Behaviour 9*, 3, 171–194.

Finkelhor, D. (1984) *Child Sexual Abuse: New Theory and Research*. New York: Free Press.

Finkelhor, D. (1994) 'Current information on the scope and nature of child sexual abuse.' *Future Child 4*, 2, 31–53.

Griffin, J. and Tyrrell, I. (2001) *The Shackled Brain: How to Release Locked-in Patterns of Trauma*. Hailsham: HG Publishing.

Griffin, J. and Tyrrell, I. (2006) *Human Givens: The New Approach to Emotional Health and Clear Thinking*. Hailsham: HG Publishing.

Gullotta, T.P. *et al.*(eds.), *Handbook of Adolescent Behavioral Problems: Evidence – Based Approaches to Prevention and Treatment*, DOI 10.1007/978-114899-7497-6_31,© Springer Science+Business Media New York 2015

Harry, J. (1992) 'Conceptualising Anti-Gay Violence.' In G. Herek and K. Berrill (eds) *Hate Crimes: Confronting Violence against Lesbians and Gay Men*. Newbury Park, CA: Sage Publications.

HM Government (n.d.) *Protection of Children Act 1978* www.legislation.gov.uk/ukpga/1978/37

Horowitz, M., Wilner, N. and Alvarez, W. (1979) 'Impact of event scale: a measure of subjective stress.' *Psychosomatic Medicine 41*, 209–218.

Lipscomb, G.H. (1992) 'Male victims of sexual assault.' *Journal of the American Medical Association 267*, 22, 3064–3066.

Porter, E. (1986) *Treating the Young Male Victims of Sexual Assault*. Syracuse, NY: Safer Society Press.

Silovsky, J.F. and Bonner, B.L. (2003) 'Children with Sexual Behaviour Problems.' In T.H. Ollendick and C.S. Schroeder (eds) *Encyclopaedia of Clinical Child and Paediatric Psychology*. New York: Kluwer Press.

References

Index